CONTENTS

A NOTE ON THIS EDITION

As no original scripts were available for the two films published in this volume, the versions presented here were built up from a dialogue continuity provided by Universal City Studios Inc., amplified with material gained from a shot-by-shot viewing of each film.

ACKNOWLEDGMENTS

Acknowledgments and thanks are due to Rank Film Distributors, the BBC and the National Film Archive for providing prints of the films, and to Bo Johan Hultman and Allen Eyles for providing stills.

CREDITS:

Screenplay by	S. J. Perelman and Will B. Johnstone
Additional dialogue by	Arthur Sheekman
Directed by	Norman McLeod
Director of photography	Arthur L. Todd
Running time	77 minutes
First shown	19 September, 1931

CAST:

The stowaways	Groucho
	Harpo
	Chico
	Zeppo
Lucille	Thelma Todd
Joe Helton	Rockliffe Fellowes
Gibson	Tom Kennedy
Mary Helton	Ruth Hall
Alky Briggs	Harry Woods
The Captain	Ben Taggart
Officer	Otto Fries
Manicurist	Evelyn Pierce
Madame Swempski	Maxine Castle

On the surface of a slowly revolving wooden barrel, the opening credits appear.

Then four more barrels in turn come rolling down a ship's gangplank and fill the screen, showing the credits for GROUCHO, HARPO, CHICO and ZEPPO MARX. The last barrel turns to show the names of the rest of the cast.

Fade out and in to a shot of an ocean liner ploughing through the waves, then dissolve to the deck of the liner, where the CAPTAIN is standing at the rail with a pair of binoculars. Some passengers are chatting in the background. First Officer GIBSON runs up with a note in his hand.

CAPTAIN : *What is it?*

GIBSON saluting : *Sorry to have to report there are four stowaways in the forward hatch.*

CAPTAIN : *Stowaways? How do you know there are four of 'em?*

GIBSON : *Why, they were singing ' Sweet Adeline '.*

CAPTAIN : *Well get them out of there, you hear?*

GIBSON : *But we can't find 'em. And besides, they've been writing insulting notes.*

He hands the note to the CAPTAIN.

CAPTAIN reading the note : *So I'm an old goat, am I?* . . . GIBSON, looking over his shoulder, nods . . . *Listen to me — find them if you have to clear out that whole hatch.*

GIBSON saluting : *Yes, sir.*

He runs off while the CAPTAIN, furious, looks out to sea through his binoculars. A girl passenger comes up to him.

GIRL brightly : *Oh, Captain, when do we get in?*

CAPTAIN snapping at her : *Wednesday!* She winces. *Oh, I . . . I beg your pardon. Wednesday.*

GIRL : *I thank you.* She starts to go off.

Down in the forward hatch, camera tracks in on four large barrels labelled KIPPERED HERRING. Voices issue from inside, singing in close harmony.

7

Zeppo off : ' *In all my dreams . . .*'
All off : ' *In all my dreams . . .*'
Zeppo off : ' *Your fair face beams . . .*'
All off : ' *Your fair face beams . . .*
        You're the idol of my heart
        Sweet Adeline.*'
Groucho off : ' *My Ad-e-line.*'

Groucho, Harpo, Chico and Zeppo lift the lids, rise from the barrels and take a bow.

Harpo, in close-up, brushes his hair with a boot brush.

Groucho off : *Ah, this is the only way to travel, boys . . . the only way.*

Now we see the four of them, with Groucho cleaning his teeth, Chico buffing his nails, while Zeppo reads a book.

Groucho : *I was gonna bring along the wife and kiddies but the grocer couldn't spare another barrel.*

Harpo drops into his barrel, and we cut to Chico and Groucho.

Chico : *I was goin' ta bring my grandfather, but there's no room*

for his beard.

GROUCHO waving his toothbrush : *Why don't you send for the old swine and let his beard come later?*

CHICO : *I sent for his beard.*

GROUCHO : *You did?*

CHICO : *Yeah, it's coming by hairmail.*

ZEPPO off : *Sssh!*

Back to the group.

ZEPPO : *Say, fellas, I think I hear someone.*

GROUCHO : *Well, if it's the Captain, I'm gonna have a few words with him.*

Cut to him and CHICO.

GROUCHO : *My hot water's been cold for three days and I haven't got room enough in here to swing a cat. In fact I haven't even got a cat.*

Resume on all three.

CHICO : *My grandfather can swing a cat.*

GROUCHO : *Yeah?*

CHICO : *Hey, that'd make a good job for him.*

GROUCHO : *Yes.*

GIBSON off : *Come on, men.*

ZEPPO : *Hey, someone's coming.*

They drop hastily into the barrels as we cut to GIBSON entering in the background with some sailors.

GIBSON : *Come on, now, snap it up. Listen, fellows . . .*

We see them come round and stand in front of the barrels.

GIBSON : *We've gotta find those stowaways, and when we do we'll put 'em in irons.*

A SAILOR saluting : *Aye, aye, sir.*

The others go off.

GIBSON pointing : *Take a look in behind those cases. You fellows look behind those boxes.* He exits.

The remaining sailor, in close-up, bends down and listens at HARPO's barrel.

GIBSON stands with his back turned beyond the barrels, as GROUCHO pops out of his.

GROUCHO : *Never mind the barrels.* He drops into his barrel.

Back by HARPO's barrel, the sailor springs to attention.

SAILOR saluting : *Aye, aye, sir!*

9

GIBSON turns in bewilderment.

GIBSON : *What's that?*

SAILOR : *I just said ' Aye, aye, sir '.*

GIBSON : *Never mind that. Find those men.*

SAILOR : *Aye, aye, sir.* He goes off.

> GIBSON turns his back again, peering to and fro. The Marx brothers rise from their barrels, then pop back again, slamming the lids. GIBSON whips round, then goes off.
>
> Seen from behind, GIBSON hurries to another part of the hold. HARPO rises from his barrel in close-up, chewing.
>
> GIBSON hears a noise and goes off in the wrong direction.
>
> HARPO scratches his chin with his hooter. It makes a noise and he drops hurriedly into the barrel.
>
> GIBSON, walking away, hears the noise and turns.
>
> Resume on the barrels as he hurries back and stands with his back to them, hands on hips. A sailor enters.

SAILOR : *They're not here, sir.*

> A closer shot of the two of them.

GIBSON : *Oh, yes they are. Hoist all this stuff up on deck. Get these barrels out of the way.*

SAILOR : *Very well, sir.* He exits.

> Back to the scene, as GIBSON pulls out a whistle and signals to the derrick operator up on deck.

GIBSON : *Lower away up there.*

> The sailors roll the barrels into position as the hoist appears from above.
>
> GIBSON, in medium close-up, points at the barrels.

GIBSON : *Hurry up with that sling.*

> Back to GIBSON and the sailors as they start to put a rope sling round the barrels.
>
> Another officer comes up to some sailors who are standing about watching.

OFFICER : *Well, you'll never find 'em standing around this way!*

SAILOR : *Yes, sir.*

OFFICER pointing : *Now you look in those bales. You look in those boxes.*

SAILOR : *Yes, sir.*

> Resume on the barrels.

GIBSON : *All right, boys.*

10

Seen from above, he shouts up to the derrick operator.

GIBSON : *Make it snappy up there.*

Back to the barrels as they are hoisted out of shot, revealing GROUCHO, CHICO, HARPO and ZEPPO squatting on the floor with their belongings. GIBSON has his back to them and starts to walk away.

In a closer shot, he starts to climb a companion way, then turns and sees . . .

The four Marx brothers squatting on the floor.

GIBSON can't believe his eyes . . .

And seen from his point of view the Marx brothers turn as he shouts :

GIBSON off : *Hey!*

They run for it, leaving their belongings as GIBSON gives chase in the background.

GIBSON : *There they are!*

Seen from behind, they run past some bales.

CHICO : *Hurry! Hurry!*

GIBSON and the sailors give chase.

CHICO, GROUCHO, ZEPPO and HARPO start up a flight of stairs . . .

While the sailors run past the bales in pursuit.

Resume on the stairs as HARPO, last up, looks back and sounds his hooter. Then GIBSON and the sailors reach the bottom and start up.

We see the Marx brothers again arriving at the top of the stairs. Some passengers watch in bewilderment as they chase off . . .

While down below the sailors run up the stairs after them.

Long shot of the crowded promenade deck. There is a general hum of voices as the Marx brothers pelt towards us, HARPO bowling a lifebelt along the floor. He drops it over a passenger's head as they run off.

Meanwhile GIBSON and the sailors reach the top of the stairs and look from side to side . . .

They charge along the promenade deck in a body, scattering the passengers.

GROUCHO, CHICO, HARPO and ZEPPO run down the staircase into the main saloon. Camera follows as they race once round

11

the fountain at the bottom, then across to the piano, where they grab up some instruments and break into a swinging jazz number, brash and out of tune. There is loud applause as they finish with a flourish, then we cut to long shot as they race out of the saloon again, the sailors thundering after them.

Back on the promenade deck, they take refuge behind some passengers sitting in deck chairs.

Camera moves with GIBSON and the sailors as they come running up and halt in front of the deck chairs. GIBSON issues orders.

GIBSON pointing: *You fellows go there. You fellows take a look in behind those lifeboats.*

The sailors run off. GIBSON paces to and fro, oblivious, as ZEPPO sneaks away behind him, while GROUCHO stands in a corner with a rug over his head. Then he turns and looks suspiciously at the occupant of one of the deck chairs.

It is CHICO in a woman's hat; seen in close-up, he coyly picks his teeth.

Resume on the scene as GIBSON leans towards him, turns away, then does a double take. CHICO runs for it and GIBSON gives chase.

A woman sitting in another deck chair rises, revealing a grinning HARPO beneath her. She screams.

Back to the scene as she runs off. HARPO rises and does likewise, while another passenger emerges from the depths of the deck chair, looking crushed. GROUCHO runs past amid the general confusion.

We now see the CAPTAIN about to go into his quarters; he is stopped by a group of girls.

GIRL eagerly: *Oh, Captain, tell us about the stowaways.*

CAPTAIN bragging: *Oh, I'll have them in the brig before long.*

GIRL: *Oh, that's terribly romantic. I'd love to meet a stowaway.* She laughs.

Suddenly GROUCHO slides down a companion way and lands beside the group. He starts back up the stairs, but the CAPTAIN stops him.

CAPTAIN: *Hey, you!*

GROUCHO holds out his gloved hands.

GROUCHO: *Are these your gloves? I found 'em in your trunk.* To the girls: *You girls go to your rooms. I'll be down shortly.*

The girls exit meekly.

CAPTAIN: *Who are you?*

GROUCHO ignoring the question: *Are you the floorwalker on this ship?*

CAPTAIN indignantly: *Floor . . .!*

GROUCHO: *If you are . . .*

A closer shot of the two of them.

GROUCHO: *. . . I want to register a complaint.*

CAPTAIN: *Why, what's the matter?*

GROUCHO: *Matter enough. Do you know who sneaked into my stateroom at three o'clock this morning?*

CAPTAIN: *Who did that?*

GROUCHO: *Nobody, and that's my complaint. I'm young. I want gaiety, laughter, ha-cha-cha.*

He breaks into a dance step, seen in a wider angle.

GROUCHO: *I want to dance. I want to dance till the cows come home.*

13

1325-101

14

CAPTAIN : *Just what do you mean by this?*

Resume on the previous shot.

GROUCHO : *Another thing. I don't care for the way you're running this boat. Why don't you get in the back seat for a while and let your wife drive.* He walks away, puffing at his cigar.

CAPTAIN : *I want you to know I've been Captain of this ship for twenty-two years.*

GROUCHO coming back : *Twenty-two years, eh? If you were a man, you'd go into business for yourself. I know a fella who started only last year with just a canoe. Now he's got more women than you could shake a stick at, if that's your idea of a good time.*

Back to the wider angle.

CAPTAIN : *One more word out of you and I'll throw you in irons.*

GROUCHO sits in a deck chair and puts his feet up.

GROUCHO : *You can't do it with irons. It's a mashie shot.*

Seen in medium close-up, he gets up and comes back towards the CAPTAIN.

GROUCHO : *It's a mashie shot if the wind is against you, and if the wind isn't, I am . . . And how about those barrels down below?*

CAPTAIN : *Barrels?*

GROUCHO indignantly : *Yeah. I wouldn't put a pig in one of those barrels.*

CAPTAIN getting angry : *Now, see here, you . . .*

GROUCHO : *No, not even if you got down on your knees.* He holds out the gloves. *And here's your gloves.* Snatching them away again : *You would take them, wouldn't you?*

He turns towards the door of the chartroom behind him.

Close-up of the CAPTAIN.

CAPTAIN hands on hips : *Why you . . .*

Resume on GROUCHO in the door of the chartroom.

GROUCHO : *And keep away from my office.*

Back to the scene as he goes in and shuts the door.

CAPTAIN : *Now, see here, you . . .*

The CAPTAIN starts forward angrily and pulls open the door. Simultaneously, CHICO slides down the companion way behind him, dodges under his arm and goes in.

Reverse shot inside the CAPTAIN's quarters. CHICO comes in, slams the door and hides behind a chair, while GROUCHO puts on an officer's coat and cap. The door opens and the CAPTAIN

15

comes in; he looks round suspiciously and crosses to another door, GROUCHO loping after him with his cap on sideways. The CAPTAIN goes into the next room and shuts the door.

GROUCHO, in medium shot, locks the door and turns to CHICO behind him.

GROUCHO : *How dare you invade the sanctity of the Captain's quarters?*

CHICO laughing : *I thought he was the Captain. Hey, I'm hungry. I'm a-lookin' for somet'ing to eat.* He opens a cupboard.

GROUCHO : *I'll take care of that.*

Seen in close-up, he picks up a phone.

GROUCHO into the phone : *Hello. Send up the Captain's lunch.*

CHICO over his shoulder : *Hey, two.*

GROUCHO : *Send up his dinner too. Who am I?* He takes off his cap, looks at the braid and puts it on again. *I'm the Captain. You want to choose up sides?*

Another shot as he puts back the phone and picks up the engine room intercom.

GROUCHO : *Oh engineer, will you tell 'em to stop the boat from*

rocking? I'm gonna have lunch.

He taps his cigar ash into the speaking tube, then turns to CHICO, who is still rummaging around just behind him. They both face camera.

GROUCHO : *Well, what's the matter with you?*

CHICO : *What's the matter with me? I'm hungry. I didn't eat in three days.*

GROUCHO : *Three days? We've only been on the boat two days.*

CHICO counting on his fingers : *Well, I didn't eat yesterday, I didn't eat today, and I'm not goin' to eat tomorrow. That makes three days.*

GROUCHO : *Well, state your business. I've got to shiver my timbers.* He hums a tune.

Seen in a longer shot, he dances a hornpipe, humming.

CHICO : *I got no business. I come up to see the Captain's bridge.*

GROUCHO : *The Captain's bridge? I'm sorry, he always keeps it in a glass of water while he's eating.* He takes CHICO's hand and leads him towards the locked door. *Would you like to see where he sleeps?*

CHICO not interested : *Aw, I saw that. That'sa the bunk.*

GROUCHO : *You're just wasting your breath, and that's no great loss, either. A fine sailor you are.*

We follow them to the chart table in the centre of the room.

CHICO sits on a corner of the table, GROUCHO on a chair.

CHICO : *Hmm, you bet I'm a fine sailor. You know my whole family was a-sailors? My father was a-partners with Columbus.*

GROUCHO : *Well, what do you think of that, eh? Your father and Columbus were partners?*

CHICO : *You bet.*

GROUCHO : *Columbus has been dead for four hundred years.*

CHICO : *Well, they told me it was my father.*

GROUCHO : *Well now, just hop up there little Johnny, and I'll show you a few things you don't know about history. Now look . . .*

CHICO sits up on the table as GROUCHO gets up and reaches for a globe.

They are seen in a closer shot.

GROUCHO drawing a circle on the globe : *Now, there's Columbus.*

CHICO pointing at it : *That'sa Columbus Circle.*

GROUCHO : *Would you mind getting up off that flypaper and giving*

17

the flies a chance?

CHICO lifts his backside off the table, sees he is sitting on a newspaper and grins.

CHICO : *Aw, you're crazy. Flies can't read papers.*

GROUCHO pointing to the globe again : *Now, Columbus sailed from Spain to India looking for a short cut.*

CHICO : *Oh, you mean strawberry short cut.*

GROUCHO takes off his cap and rubs his head.

GROUCHO : *I don't know. When I woke up, there was the nurse taking care of me.*

CHICO : *What's the matter? Couldn't the nurse take care of herself?*

GROUCHO : *You bet she could, but I found her out too late. Well, enough of this. Let's get back to Columbus.* He puts on his cap again.

CHICO : *I'd rather get back to the nurse.*

GROUCHO drawing on the globe : *So would I. But Columbus was sailing along on his vessel . . .*

CHICO : *On his what?*

GROUCHO : *Not on his what — on his vessel. Don't you know what vessel is?*

CHICO : *Sure. I can vessel.*

He whistles the tune of ' Sugar in the morning . . .'. GROUCHO throws down his pencil in disgust. CHICO gets off the table and goes out of shot.

GROUCHO : *Do you suppose I could buy back my introduction to you?*

A medium shot includes CHICO again as he sits in a chair on the other side of the table. GROUCHO resumes his discourse.

GROUCHO : *Now, one night Columbus' sailors started a mutiny . . .*

CHICO : *Naw, no mutinies at night. They're in the afternoon. You know, mutinies Wednesdays and Saturdays.*

GROUCHO throwing down his cap : *There's my argument. Restrict immigration.*

Silhouetted against the glass partition behind them, GIBSON comes down the companion way and pauses outside the door. GROUCHO and CHICO exit under the table.

GIBSON opens the door, looking over his shoulder . . .

He comes into the chartroom . . .

He turns, in close-up, and finds the room apparently empty.

Under the table, Groucho and Chico watch over their shoulders as Gibson's legs exit in the background, then they turn towards camera, grinning.

Resume on the scene. Chico and Groucho rise from under the table as a waiter comes in through the door, carrying a tray. They follow him across to the door of the Captain's cabin, mimicking him with upturned palms.

Inside the Captain's cabin, the waiter enters and sets the tray down on the table. Groucho and Chico hover in the doorway, then stride into the room, as the Captain dismisses the waiter and sits down at the table.

Captain to the waiter : *All right.*

Groucho sits down at table with the Captain, while Chico stands opposite. The Captain is amazed.

Captain : *Well, of all the colossal impudence!*

Groucho removes the napkin from the lunch tray.

Groucho : *Why can't you stand up? Can't you see he has no chair?*

Chico pulls up a chair and sits down, while Groucho tucks the napkin into his collar.

19

CAPTAIN speechless: *Why ... ugh ... you ...!*
CHICO, in medium close-up, grabs his table napkin.
CHICO: *You better keep quiet. We're a coupla big stockholders in this company.*
Resume on the three men at table.
CAPTAIN: *Stockholders, huh? Well, you look like a couple of stowaways to me.*
GROUCHO standing up: *Well don't forget, my fine fellow, that the stockholder of yesteryear is the stowaway of today.*
CAPTAIN: *Well, you look exactly like 'em.*
CHICO: *Yeah? What do they look like?*
Close-up of the CAPTAIN. He looks meaningfully at GROUCHO.
CAPTAIN: *One of them goes around with a black moustache.*
Camera on GROUCHO.
GROUCHO: *So do I. If I had my choice I'd go around with a little blonde.* He waggles his eyebrows.
Back to the CAPTAIN.
CAPTAIN with emphasis: *I said, one goes around with a black moustache!*
Resume on GROUCHO.
GROUCHO: *Well, you couldn't expect a moustache to go around by itself.*
Pan to include the CAPTAIN. GROUCHO lays a hand on his arm.
GROUCHO coyly: *Don't you think a moustache ever gets lonely, Captain?*
Resume on the scene as the CAPTAIN shrugs him off.
CHICO: *Hey, sure it gets-a lonely. Hey, when my grandfather's beard gets here, I'd like it to meet your moustache.*
GROUCHO is seen in medium close-up.
GROUCHO: *Well, I'll think it over. I'll talk it over with my moustache.* He leans forward. *Tell me, has your grandfather's beard got any money?*
CHICO: *Money? Why, he fell hair to a fortune.*
Back to the scene as the CAPTAIN rises indignantly.
CAPTAIN: *Now listen, stockholders or no stockholders, you clear out of here.*
The others rise also.
GROUCHO: *All right.*
Sound of knocking, off.

20

CHICO : *Hey! Maybe there's somebody in that room.*

GROUCHO pointing : *There's somebody in that closet there* . . .
The CAPTAIN hurries across the cabin, followed by CHICO and
GROUCHO.

GROUCHO : . . . *And I think it's you, Captain.*
They push him into the closet and lock the door.*
Out on deck, GIBSON comes down the companion way by the
chartroom door and looks from side to side.
Meanwhile, inside the CAPTAIN's cabin, GROUCHO and CHICO
settle down to their meal.

GROUCHO : *Well, now we can eat in peace.*

CHICO : *All right. Here's a piece for you.*

GROUCHO : *Atta boy.*
There is a knock at the door and GIBSON hurries in in the
background. GROUCHO springs to his feet, turning his back on
him, and puts on his captain's cap.

GIBSON saluting : *Beg pardon, Captain* . . .
Medium close-up of GROUCHO.

---

* In the National Film Archive print, the scene between MARY and ZEPPO,
which comes a little later, is inserted at this point.

GROUCHO eyebrows working: *How dare you enter the Captain's quarters while I'm eating!*
Resume on the scene.
GIBSON saluting: *Sorry, sir.*
He goes towards the door, while GROUCHO sits down, laughing, and shakes hands with CHICO across the table. At that moment there is thunderous knocking from the imprisoned CAPTAIN off-screen.
Seen by the door, GIBSON turns and comes forward again, peering through his spectacles.
Resume on the scene.
GIBSON: *Now I got you!*
He chases them round the table, GROUCHO and CHICO grabbing up the food as they go.
CHICO: *Don't forget the butter.*
They run for the door.

The scene changes to a corridor by the cloakrooms. HARPO is leaning against a sign which reads MEN on the wall. A

man comes up, looks at the sign and goes into the cloakroom, then reappears, catapulted through the door. He gets up, peers from the sign to HARPO, then hurries off in bewilderment. HARPO moves to reveal the entire sign, which now reads WOMEN. At that moment a chambermaid passes down the corridor. HARPO grins and starts off after her as the chambermaid takes to her heels.

Seen from behind, HARPO chases her down the corridor.

On the promenade deck, ZEPPO skids past and through a doorway with GIBSON in hot pursuit. He reappears through another glass door and crouches down, hiding from GIBSON, as a girl — MARY — walks through. ZEPPO springs up and strolls along beside her, taking her by the arm. Camera tracks ahead of them.

ZEPPO expansively : *You know, there's some mighty pretty country round here. I've . . .*

MARY : *I beg your pardon?*

She disengages herself and walks on. ZEPPO strides ahead of her whistling. He drops his handkerchief, picks it up, and steps up to MARY again.

ZEPPO : *Pardon me, is this yours?*

MARY : *Why no.*

She walks on. ZEPPO hesitates, then tries again.

ZEPPO : *Are you sure?*

MARY sweetly : *I'm positive.*

A smile comes over her face as she walks on. She drops her own handkerchief and waits. Then as ZEPPO hurries up again she picks it up and holds it out to him.

MARY : *Is this yours?*

ZEPPO pocketing the handkerchief : *Yes, it is.* He takes her by the arms and they stroll on. *Well, as I was saying, there's some mighty beautiful country round here.*

MARY enthusiastically : *The trees are lovely.*

ZEPPO : *Oh, you bet they are. I love 'em.*

They go off in the foreground.

The scene changes to another corridor. HARPO runs up to a door.

Inside is the nursery, where the children are watching a Punch and Judy show. We hear squeaking voices and laughter, as HARPO runs in through the door and hides beside the Punch and Judy booth.

In a closer shot, he looks up and notices the puppets. Grinning from ear to ear, he goes to sit with the children and settles down to enjoy the show.

In the corridor outside, GIBSON runs up to the nursery door.

We see him come in through the door, then cut to HARPO, who takes refuge inside the Punch and Judy booth.

Camera moves with GIBSON as he hurries across the room, almost knocking over a child.

GIBSON to the child: *Get out of my way.*

He stands in front of the booth, peering to and fro, while HARPO's head appears between Punch and Judy.

In a closer shot, GIBSON walks to and fro in front of the booth; then he peers myopically at the puppets and taps Punch on the nose to see if he's real. Punch and Judy hit HARPO on the head with their sticks, and the children shout with glee.

PUNCH: *Whoopee! Whoopee!*

HARPO slaps GIBSON's face from behind, then dodges down out of sight. GIBSON whips round and peers down into the booth. Shot of the scene as he goes round the side.

Round the back, HARPO's backside protrudes between the curtains as GIBSON appears.

HARPO's face is seen between Punch and Judy, rocking to and fro.

Resume on GIBSON, who has an idea.

Seen in close-up, he removes his tie-pin . . .

And jabs it into HARPO's backside.

HARPO, between Punch and Judy, screams with pain.

GIBSON grabs a cricket bat and hurries round the front, while HARPO's face emerges at the back.

His backside is now protruding between the front curtains; GIBSON swipes it with the cricket bat.

And HARPO, eyes bulging, blows a squeaker.

Resume on the scene from the front. Punch and Judy watch as GIBSON drops the bat and goes inside the booth.

Seen in close-up the puppets disappear, while GIBSON pops up, throttling HARPO.

24

The children in the audience shout and scream with glee, laughing and applauding the show.

At that moment the door opens and the CAPTAIN enters, led by a little girl and smiling benignly.

Close-up of GIBSON in the booth, throttling HARPO.

The CAPTAIN sees them, his smile fades, and he calls out sternly :

CAPTAIN : *Gibson!*

GIBSON releases HARPO and looks round.

Resume on the CAPTAIN

CAPTAIN : *Come out of there!*

We now see him standing in front of the booth, with GIBSON and HARPO inside.

GIBSON : *Yes, sir.*

He disappears from view, then emerges from the booth.

GIBSON : *I want to report I found a . . .*

CAPTAIN : *Gibson, you've been drinking again and you know what my orders were.*

Behind them HARPO disappears and Punch bobs up in his place.

GIBSON : *But those stowaways — I just caught one of them in there.*
CAPTAIN : *Stowaways, huh?*
GIBSON turning : *Yes. There he is.*
> Cut to medium shot as he grabs Punch by the neck.
PUNCH squeaking : *Ouch! Look out, you're choking me. Look out!*
> The CAPTAIN taps Punch's nose; it makes a hollow sound.
CAPTAIN to GIBSON : *I thought so. Go to your quarters.*
> Behind them, HARPO replaces Punch again, and blows his squeaker at the CAPTAIN as he turns away.
> In a closer shot, HARPO whips round, revealing a false face on the back of his head. The audience shout with glee, while the CAPTAIN reappears.
GIBSON : *That's him now.*
CAPTAIN tapping the mask : *That's a dummy. Come with me.*
> He exits as HARPO turns and blows the squeaker at GIBSON. Laughter. GIBSON taps HARPO's face.
> Back to the scene as HARPO whips round, showing the mask again. The CAPTAIN, who has started for the door, comes back towards the booth.
CAPTAIN sternly : *First Officer!*
GIBSON : *I'm telling you that's him!*
CAPTAIN : *This has gone far enough. Get up to your quarters.*
> GIBSON goes past him, then HARPO turns and kicks the CAPTAIN through the front of the booth.
CAPTAIN : *Oh!*
> GIBSON whips round and salutes.
GIBSON : *Yes, sir.*
> Laughter off.
CAPTAIN to the children : *Quiet!*
> He pokes HARPO's cheek, then says to GIBSON :
CAPTAIN : *I think you're right.*
> HARPO kicks him again, and this time the CAPTAIN grabs his leg and pulls.
CAPTAIN : *I know you're right!*
PUNCH reappearing next to HARPO : *Look out there. What're you doing? What're you doing?*
> In the audience, the children shout and clap with glee.
> Back to the scene as the CAPTAIN and GIBSON both start heaving at HARPO's leg. The children laugh and Punch

26

squeaks, while HARPO whistles encouragement. Suddenly, he disappears from the booth, emerges behind GIBSON and starts heaving with the other two. The false leg finally gives way and they collapse in a heap on the floor.

HARPO goes into the booth again . . .

He reappears on the other side, where the Crocodile is now visible, its jaws flapping. He picks up his hat and hooter from a chair.

We see the CAPTAIN and GIBSON on the floor, embracing the false leg . . .

Then resume on HARPO. He sticks the bulb of the hooter between the Crocodile's jaws; it sounds the hooter.

At the side of the room, he gets onto a kiddy-car and rides it down a track towards the door; the camera follows and the children scream with glee.

Seen from behind, he trundles off down the corridor, the mask still fixed to the back of his head. Two passengers skip out of the way as he signals a left turn and rounds the corner, sounding his hooter.

In the barber's shop, CHICO is sitting in a chair, being given a manicure by a blonde manicurist. The BARBER comes up.

BARBER : *Er — would you like to have anything before lunch?*

CHICO : *Yes, breakfast.*

BARBER : *Why, nobody eats in here.*

CHICO gets out a sandwich.

CHICO : *I do.* He takes a bite and makes a face. *Mustard's no good without roast beef.*

He throws the sandwich away and the BARBER exits.

MANICURIST : *Do you want your nails trimmed long?*

CHICO : *Oh, about an hour and a half. I got nothin' to do.* He grins. *Hey, you're a nice-a lookin' gal, all right. You got it.*

MANICURIST smiling : *Thank you.*

CHICO : *And you can keep it.*

There are noises off as we cut to a medium shot of the doorway. HARPO trundles up on his kiddy-car, hits the door sill and falls to the floor. He hides his head under the carpet as GIBSON thunders past outside.

In a closer shot, HARPO looks out from under the rug, sees

27

CHICO and grins.

Resume on the scene as CHICO approaches with the MANI-
CURIST. HARPO gets up, holds up his mask and pulls a face.
The MANICURIST screams and runs off.

A closer shot of CHICO and HARPO.

CHICO : *Yeah, that's a nice girl, hey?*

In the corridor outside, the SECOND OFFICER approaches. He
has a luxuriant moustache.

Back to HARPO and CHICO.

CHICO : *Somebody's comin'!*

They exit.

In the corridor, the OFFICER reaches the door of the barber's
shop and beckons to some sailors.

OFFICER : *Come on, boys.*

The sailors appear and follow him in.

Inside, HARPO and CHICO are standing by the chair in barber's
aprons as the OFFICER and sailors enter. HARPO whistles and
CHICO says :

CHICO : *You're next, Cap.*

OFFICER : *Say, I'm looking for a couple of mugs.*

HARPO holds out a couple of shaving mugs.

OFFICER : *No, no!* To the sailors : *Say, you boys look on B deck.*

SAILORS : *Aye, aye, sir.* They go off.

Medium shot of the three of them.

CHICO : *Well, how about a shave, huh?*

OFFICER : *Sure. Gimme a once-over.*

CHICO to HARPO : *Once over, partner.*

They crouch on either side of the OFFICER and HARPO whistles,
indicating a somersault.

OFFICER tapping his face : *No, a shave.*

CHICO : *On the face. All right.*

The OFFICER gets into the chair and says :

OFFICER : *Say, wake me up when you get through.*

CHICO : *You bet.*

A closer shot, with the OFFICER seated in the chair.

CHICO taking his cap : *We take care of you, all right.*

The OFFICER yawns hugely and shuts his eyes. HARPO ties him
to the chair with an apron, while CHICO grabs a cut-throat
razor and looks down his throat.

28

CHICO : *We take-a the tonsils last. I think we work the moustache first . . . Give 'im a little snoop.*

HARPO *brandishes the scissors.*

In a medium close-up, camera follows HARPO as he moves to and fro. He cuts a piece off one side of the OFFICER's moustache, then stands back to admire the effect.

CHICO off at first : *This side's too long. Give 'im a little snoop this side.*

HARPO *snips a piece off the other side.*

CHICO : *Now this side's too short.*

HARPO looks indignant and makes as if to cut the same side again.

CHICO : *It's too short. The other side is too long. Snoop 'im up.*

HARPO cuts far too much off the other side.

Shot of CHICO as he stands back to inspect HARPO's handiwork.

CHICO : *That's better, but the side's too short now is too long, the side's too long is too short . . . I think we gotta give 'im one more snoop.*

Resume on the three of them as HARPO takes too much off the other side again, then cut to a shot of the scene.

CHICO : *I think we better measure.*

They both grab tape measures, measure a yard or so out from the OFFICER's moustache and compare lengths. CHICO points at HARPO's measure.

CHICO : *It's about a foot too much.*

HARPO grabs a hammer and the OFFICER's foot.

CHICO restraining him : *Hey, no! The measure's about a foot too much!*

HARPO cuts a foot off the tape measure.

Shot of CHICO.

CHICO : *Now, looks much better.*

Close-up of HARPO and the OFFICER.

CHICO off : *It can stand one more snoop in the middle, I think . . .*

HARPO looks bewildered : *. . . In the middle, one snoop.*

HARPO snips the moustache straight across; it is now no more than a toothbrush.

CHICO off : *'At'sa fine.* He laughs. *'At'sa very good.*

HARPO looks pleased, and we cut to CHICO, pointing.

CHICO : *I think — I think it's a little bit rough right here . . . Pan* to include the OFFICER . . . *I fix that.*

We now see HARPO stropping a razor on the shower tube by the basin.

CHICO off : *You know, I'm never goin' on this boat again. The food's no good.*

HARPO slices up a block of wood, testing the razor.

CHICO off : *Of course, I don't eat yet, but even if I don't eat I like the food good.*

HARPO whistles, satisfied, and strops the razor once more on the marble counter.

Back to the scene. CHICO has now lathered the OFFICER's moustache.

CHICO : *One more snoop.*

HARPO wields the razor and CHICO wipes away the lather.

CHICO : *Hah! 'At'sa beautiful, hey! 'At'sa what you call a work of art.*

He peers more closely. HARPO has shaved off the whole moustache.

CHICO : *Hey, you know, I think you give 'im one snoop too much.*

We move to the stateroom occupied by ALKY BRIGGS and his wife LUCILLE. BRIGGS sits pulling on his spats while LUCILLE paces angrily to and fro.

Seen in medium shot, she comes and stands over him.

LUCILLE : *And I want you to know, I'm fed up with your alibis.*

BRIGGS : *Aw, take it easy. You're getting all excited.*

He gets up and takes his hat from the table.

LUCILLE hands on hips : *Now where do you think you're going?*

BRIGGS : *Never mind. I'm running this racket. Just stay here and keep out of sight like I told you.*

He walks to the door; she runs in front and stops him.

LUCILLE : *Oh no, you don't.*

The two of them are seen in medium close-up, LUCILLE with her back to the door.

LUCILLE : *Now listen to me, Mr. Alky Briggs. You can't keep me cooped up like this. I've played second fiddle on this ship long enough.*

BRIGGS pulls her away from the door.

BRIGGS : *Now you listen. I'm not after any dames. I'm after Joe*

Helton, I tell you, and he can't get away from me on this boat . . .
LUCILLE folds her arms . . . *He's gonna put his okay on my gang or he's gonna get this.* He taps his pocket.

Out on the promenade deck, GIBSON spots GROUCHO in a deck chair and gives chase. GROUCHO shoves the chair in GIBSON's way, tripping him up, and runs off.

In the corridor outside BRIGGS's stateroom, GROUCHO runs towards camera but skids to a halt, falling over, as he sees . . . An officer with a couple of passengers at the other end.

GROUCHO starts back in the opposite direction but skids to a halt again as GIBSON appears, blocking his exit. At that moment a tailor approaches carrying a couple of dresses on hangers, and knocks at a cabin door. GROUCHO grabs one of the dresses and, using it as a shield, makes for the door of BRIGGS's stateroom, while GIBSON spots him and follows.

GIBSON : *Hey, who are you?*

We see GROUCHO at the door.

GROUCHO : *I'm the tailor.*

Shot of GIBSON approaching.

GIBSON : *Oh! That reminds me, where are my pants?*

Resume on GROUCHO.

GROUCHO : *You've got 'em on.*

Back to GIBSON : he looks down at his pants.

Seen from inside, GROUCHO barges into the stateroom and comes face to face with BRIGGS and LUCILLE.

GROUCHO : *Er . . . pardon me while I step into the closet.*

Camera pans as he crosses to the closet and steps inside.

LUCILLE off : *And get a load of this . . .*

Resume on her and BRIGGS.

LUCILLE : *If you come in again at three o'clock in the morning, I'm going . . .*

BRIGGS : *Aw, stop bothering me. Tell it to the tailor.* He opens the door.

LUCILLE : *Alky!*

Cut to a longer shot as he goes out.

LUCILLE : *Alky!*

She takes a few paces back and hurls something at the door, then we cut to a long shot as she crosses to the closet by the bed.

We see her approaching the closet door, where she calls out:

LUCILLE : *Say, what are you doing in there?*

Cut to the door of the closet as GROUCHO opens it and sticks his head out.

GROUCHO in a whisper : *Nothing. Come on in.*

He beckons, rolling his eyes, and goes back into the closet.

Resume on LUCILLE.

LUCILLE : *You can't stay in that closet.*

GROUCHO steps out again beside her.

GROUCHO : *Oh, I can't, can I? That's what they said to Thomas Edison, mighty inventor . . . Thomas Lindberg, mighty flier, and Thomas Shefsky, mighty like a rose.* He chucks her cheek. *Just remember, my little cabbage, that if there weren't any closets, there wouldn't be any hooks, and if there weren't any hooks, there wouldn't be any fish, and that would suit me fine.*

Shot of the scene as he goes back into the closet.

LUCILLE leaning against the door : *Don't try to hide. I know you're in that closet.*

GROUCHO steps out of another door behind her.

GROUCHO : *Did you see me go in the closet?*
LUCILLE turning : *No.*
GROUCHO : *Am I in the closet now?*
LUCILLE : *Well, no.*
GROUCHO theatrically : *Then how do you know I was in the closet? Your honour, I rest my case.*
> He throws himself down on the bed.
> LUCILLE, in medium close-up, glances towards the door, then says :
LUCILLE invitingly : *Come here, brown eyes.*
> GROUCHO snuggles against the pillow.
GROUCHO : *Oh, no. You're not going to get me off this bed.*
> LUCILLE stands over him.
LUCILLE : *I didn't know you were a lawyer. You're awfully shy for a lawyer.*
> Back to GROUCHO.
GROUCHO : *You bet I'm shy. I'm a shyster lawyer.*
> Shot of the scene.
LUCILLE : *Well then, what do you think of an egg that would give me . . .*
GROUCHO sitting up : *I know, I know. You're a woman who's been getting nothing but dirty breaks.*
> Close-up of GROUCHO, with LUCILLE's bosom over him.
GROUCHO : *Well, we can clean and tighten your brakes, but you'll have to stay in the garage all night.* He lies down.
> Shot of LUCILLE.
LUCILLE : *I want excitement. I want to ha-cha-cha-cha.* She breaks into a dance step.
> Back to the scene as GROUCHO picks up a guitar and strums it while she dances. Then he throws it down and lies back again.
LUCILLE : *You don't realize it . . .*
> We see her from the end of the bed, standing over him.
LUCILLE : *. . . but from the time he got the marriage licence. I've led a dog's life.* She goes off.
GROUCHO : *Are you sure he didn't get a dog's licence?*
> Cut to show them from the side of the bed.
LUCILLE : *Oh, Alky can't make a fool of me.*
> We see them from the foot of the bed again.
LUCILLE excitedly : *I want to go places. I want to do things. I*

want freedom, I want liberty, I want justice ... She goes off.

GROUCHO trumpeting : *Ta-ra-ta-da-da* ...

He sits up as LUCILLE reappears.

GROUCHO : *Madam, you're making history. In fact, you're making me, and I wish you'd keep my hands to yourself.*

Resume on the side of the bed as GROUCHO lies down again.

LUCILLE excitedly : *Oh, you know what I want. I want life, I want laughter, I want gaiety. I want to ha-cha-cha-cha* ...

She does a dance step — he strums the guitar.

Shot of GROUCHO from the end of the bed.

GROUCHO : *Madam, before I get through with you, you will have a clear case for divorce, and so will my wife.*

Camera pans as he gets up and approaches LUCILLE.

GROUCHO : *Now, the first thing to do is to arrange for a settlement. You take the children, your husband takes the house. Junior burns down the house, you take the insurance, and I take you.* He puts his arms round her.

LUCILLE : *But I haven't any children.*

GROUCHO : *That's just the trouble with this country. You haven't*

any children, and as for me . . . Dramatically : *I'm going back in the closet, where men are empty overcoats.* He opens the door and steps in.

Cut to a longer shot.

LUCILLE : *Oh, brown eyes!*

She follows him into the closet and closes the door. GROUCHO emerges from the other door and leans against the wall.

LUCILLE comes out after him and throws herself into his arms.

GROUCHO tossing away his cigar : *Wheee!*

Loud tango music; camera pans as they dance across the room, round the table, up onto the bed and off again. They dance back to back, then LUCILLE disappears while GROUCHO cavorts solo by the door. It opens, and BRIGGS comes in.

Oblivious, GROUCHO backs up to BRIGGS, takes his hands and dances with him.

Seen in close-up, he holds up his mouth to be kissed. Then he opens his eyes and winces. The music stops, and we cut back to the two of them.

GROUCHO : *Sir, this is an outrage, breaking into a man's home. I'm not in the habit of making threats, but there'll be a letter about*

this in the Times *tomorrow morning.* He flaps his coat-tails in indignation.

BRIGGS threateningly: *Yeah? But you won't read it, 'cause I'm gonna lay you out pretty.*

GROUCHO: *Oh, you're gonna lay me out pretty, eh? That's the thanks I get for freeing an innocent girl who, although she is hiding in the closet at this moment, has promised to become the mother of her children. And with that, sir, I bid you a fond farewell. Good day, sir.*

Pan as he moves towards the closet with the utmost dignity. Shot of the stateroom.

GROUCHO: *Good day!* He exits into the closet.

BRIGGS going up to the door: *Come out of there. I want to talk to you.*

They are seen in medium close-up as GROUCHO opens the door.

GROUCHO: *I'm sorry, but we're using the old-fashioned ice man, and we find him very satisfactory for keeping the house warm.* He shuts the door.

Back to the scene as BRIGGS opens the door of the closet again. GROUCHO comes out, crouched behind a dress, and makes for the door of the stateroom.

As he gets there, BRIGGS catches him up and grabs the dress.

GROUCHO: *Just as I thought, you're yellow — grabbing a woman's skirts!*

BRIGGS throwing down the dress: *I'm wise! I'm wise!*

A closer shot of the two of them.

GROUCHO: *You're wise, eh? Well, what's the capital of Nebraska? What's the capital of the Chase National Bank? Give up?*

BRIGGS growling: *You . . .*

GROUCHO: *Now, I'll try you on an easy one. How many Frenchmen can't be wrong?*

BRIGGS: *I know, but . . .*

GROUCHO: *You were warm and so was she. But don't be discouraged . . .* He pats his arm . . . *With a little study you'll go a long way, and I wish you'd start now.*

Shot of the scene as GROUCHO turns to go. BRIGGS holds out a gun in his jacket pocket.

BRIGGS: *Do you see this gat?*

GROUCHO peers into the pocket.

GROUCHO : *Cute, isn't it? Santa Claus bring it for Christmas?*
Preening : *I got a fire engine.*
BRIGGS : *Listen, mug, do you know who I am?*
GROUCHO : *Now don't tell me.* He leans his head against the door, pondering. *Are you animal or vegetable?*
  BRIGGS growls with fury.
GROUCHO : *Animal.*
BRIGGS : *Get this. I'm Alky Briggs.*
GROUCHO taken aback : *And I . . . I'm the man who talks too much. Fancy meeting you here after all these drinks.* He slaps him on the back.
  Seen in close-up at the closet door, LUCILLE puts a finger to her lips.
  We see GROUCHO and BRIGGS again as GROUCHO blows LUCILLE a kiss.
  LUCILLE exits into the closet.
  And we resume on the scene as GROUCHO edges towards the door.
BRIGGS holding him back : *Wait a minute.*
GROUCHO : *Sorry, I can't stay. The Captain's waiting to chase me round the deck.* He turns to go.
BRIGGS brandishing the gun : *You can stay, all right, until I finish with you.*
  On his last words, we cut to LUCILLE as she runs out of the closet.
  She comes up and throws herself on BRIGGS.
LUCILLE : *Alky, darling, please . . .*
BRIGGS : *Don't ' darling ' me. Get in that next room and stay there.* She hesitates. *Get in that next room!*
  She goes off and GROUCHO starts after her, but BRIGGS stops him.
GROUCHO : *Oh, I'm not good enough for her, am I?*
  We see LUCILLE go into the next room and slam the door. Then resume on the two men.
BRIGGS : *Is there anything you've got to say before I drill ya?*
GROUCHO : *Yes, I'd like to ask you one question.*
BRIGGS : *Go ahead.*
GROUCHO coyly : *Do you think that girls think less of a boy if he lets himself be kissed?*

BRIGGS backs away and sits down as GROUCHO advances on him.

GROUCHO : *I mean, don't you think that although girls go out with boys like me — they always marry the other kind?*

He works his eyebrows. BRIGGS stares at him.

GROUCHO opening his jacket : *Well, all right, if you're gonna kill me, hurry up. I have to take my tonic at two.*

Close-up of BRIGGS.

BRIGGS amused : *Say, I could use a guy with your nerve.*

Resume on the two of them.

BRIGGS getting up : *I think we could get along well together.*

GROUCHO coyly : *Well, of course, the first year we might have our little squabbles, but then that's inevitable, don't you think?*

In the corridor outside, ZEPPO dodges away from an officer and opens the stateroom door.

We see him again as he comes into the stateroom, shuts the door and listens for sounds of pursuit, watched by GROUCHO and BRIGGS.

BRIGGS threatening : *And what do you want here?*

ZEPPO whips round at the sound of his voice and GROUCHO motions him away.

ZEPPO embarrassed : *Why, I was . . .* Indicating GROUCHO : *I was just looking for him.*

BRIGGS to GROUCHO : *Do you know this guy?*

The three of them are seen in medium shot.

GROUCHO : *Why, I've known him for years. He used to live in the barrel next to me.*

BRIGGS : *Oh, I see. The stowaways . . .* GROUCHO makes a face . . . *Say, I can help you bozos.*

GROUCHO : *Mr. Bozos to you.*

BRIGGS : *All right. Mr. Bozo. And you can help me. I'm short-handed, and I want to get a guy on this boat.*

GROUCHO : *Well, it's too late to get him on now. You should have said something before we sailed.*

BRIGGS pulls out a bit of paper.

BRIGGS : *Listen. This is a map of B deck. There's Joe Helton's stateroom . . .*

A closer shot of the three of them.

BRIGGS : *. . . and he's a tough egg. And you're coming with me* *while I have it out with Joe.*

He puts away the paper and goes off. ZEPPO crosses to GROUCHO.

ZEPPO : *Say, do you know who Joe Helton is?*

GROUCHO : *I think I'll get off this boat until this blows over.*

They make for the door but BRIGGS reappears with a couple of guns.

BRIGGS : *If you know what's good for you, you'll stick with me.* He shoves the guns into their hands. *Now, you keep the windows covered while I go in. Now move!*

Unwillingly, GROUCHO opens the door.

Seen from outside, GROUCHO and ZEPPO come out of the stateroom, looking uncertainly at their guns. BRIGGS appears in the doorway behind them.

In the corridor, a sailor is washing down a hand rail with a tub of water on the floor beside him. GROUCHO and ZEPPO drop their guns in the tub and run off, while BRIGGS comes out of the door.

Meanwhile, in the main saloon, HARPO comes up to some children playing round the fountain at the bottom of the staircase. The children shout and laugh at him, and he shoos them away. Then he looks down into the water, sounds his hooter and takes off his hat.

In a closer shot, HARPO kneels down by the fountain, holding out his hat. He whistles and sounds his hooter and a frog jumps out of the water into the hat. He gets up.

Cut to close-up as HARPO puts on his hat. The frog croaks inside it and the crown moves up and down. HARPO grins and rolls his eyes.

We move to the promenade deck as CHICO comes running towards us, looking over his shoulder. He cannons into a man, knocking him over, picks him up and dusts him down with a laugh, then rushes off in the foreground. Immediately afterwards, GIBSON appears in pursuit and knocks the same man flying again, then rushes off after CHICO.

Resume on the main saloon, where two men are sitting absorbed in a game of chess. HARPO wanders up, whistling, and sits down between them.

A closer shot as one of the men leans forward to make a move; his opponent and HARPO start forward too. However, he thinks better of it and leans back again; so do the other two. The same thing happens again, then CHICO enters and leans over them. The FIRST MAN starts to make a move again, but HARPO restrains him, shaking his head. The other man looks up.

OPPONENT indignantly : *What is the idea of this?*

CHICO : *That's all right. I make a move for you.*

He takes a white piece with a black and HARPO removes it from the board.

FIRST MAN furious : *Why, this is an outrage.*

OPPONENT : *I'll call the Captain.*

CHICO : *The Captain don't play chess.*

FIRST MAN getting up : *Purser! Purser!*

OPPONENT getting up : *Steward! Steward! Come here.*

CHICO to HARPO : *Too much noise here for us. We better go some place where it's quiet.*

Camera pans as he and HARPO pick up the chess board and start off, leaving general confusion behind them.

The scene changes to JOE HELTON's stateroom. HELTON is sitting finishing his breakfast, wearing a dressing gown and reading a newspaper. There is a knock at the door.

HELTON : *Come in.*

A steward enters with a tray.

STEWARD : Your cigars, sir.

Seen in a medium shot, HELTON takes the cigars from the tray.

HELTON : *Thank you.*

The steward picks up the breakfast tray from the table and starts to go out. HELTON gets up.

HELTON : *Wait a minute.*

He pulls out a bundle of notes and throws one down on the tray.

Resume on the scene.

STEWARD : *Oh, thank you, sir.* He starts out.

HELTON is now seen in medium close-up as he sits down and picks up the newspaper.

Close-up of the paper with the headline : MILLIONAIRE RACKETEER RETURNS TO AMERICA, then dissolve to an insert of HELTON's photograph beside it.

HELTON looks at the paper and nods with satisfaction.

In the corridor outside, MARY, the girl whom we saw with ZEPPO, approaches the door of the stateroom, back to camera. Inside the stateroom, camera pans with MARY as she comes in through the door and goes across to her father, who has now got up.

MARY pointing at his dressing gown : *Aw, Dad, now look at you. You're not even dressed yet.*

A closer shot of the two of them, as HELTON pats her on the arm.

HELTON : *You can do all the dressing for the family, Mary. Old Joe Helton is taking things easy for the rest of his life.* He sits down. *We're big shots now, baby.*

Out in the corridor, BRIGGS goes up to the door in back view. He looks furtively round, then knocks.

On the sound of the knock, we cut back to the interior of the stateroom.

HELTON : *Come in.*

42

BRIGGS comes in and HELTON gets up, holding MARY by the hand.

BRIGGS breezily : *Hello, Joe.*

HELTON unenthusiastic : *Hello, Briggs.*

A closer shot of the three of them.

HELTON : *What do you want?*

BRIGGS eyes MARY appreciatively.

BRIGGS : *Oh, I just wanted to have a friendly talk. You know, I'm sorta worried about business.*

HELTON to MARY : *Step into the other room, baby.*

MARY : *Oh, but Dad . . .*

HELTON firmly : *Run along, honey.*

MARY exits and BRIGGS turns to watch her go.

BRIGGS : *Your kid?*

We see MARY going through the door into the next room; she looks suspiciously back.

Then we resume on the two men.

BRIGGS : *She's cute, isn't she?*

HELTON : *I don't think we've got anything to talk about. Get out!*

BRIGGS : *Not before I get your okay on my gang.*

HELTON : *I'm not doing you any favours.*

BRIGGS : *Oh yes, you are . . .*

He puts his hand in his breast pocket. HELTON reaches for his gun, but BRIGGS only pulls out a bit of paper.

BRIGGS : *You're gonna sign this.* He hands it to HELTON.

In the corridor, HARPO and CHICO approach the door of the stateroom, carrying the chess board between them. A dog barks off-screen and HARPO turns angrily to silence it. CHICO motions him into the room.

Resume on the scene inside the stateroom. Engaged in their argument, HELTON and BRIGGS do not notice as HARPO and CHICO come in through the door and settle down to their chess game on the bed.

BRIGGS : *I'm taking over your territory or there's gonna be trouble.*

HELTON : *I'm taking no sides. You'll have to fight it out with Butch and the gang.*

BRIGGS loudly : *I'm stepping into your shoes as boss.*

HARPO turns and shushes BRIGGS, who has his back to him.

HELTON : *I'm not backing up any small-time chiseller.*

We see HARPO and CHICO engrossed in their game, as the argument gets fiercer off-screen.

BRIGGS off : *Aw, don't put on the Ritz with me.*

HELTON off : *Say, don't get cocky with me, Briggs.*

HARPO turns indignantly and mouths 'shut up' at the two men.

BRIGGS off : *I'm talking turkey. You can't make all the dough and then run out on your pals.*

Resume on the scene.

HELTON : *I'm not taking orders from a mug like you. Scram!*

He tears up the paper and throws it on the ground.

BRIGGS : *So that's your answer, huh? Well, here's mine . . .*

He brings up his gun in his jacket pocket, but at the same time HARPO gets up and hits him over the head with his hooter.

A closer shot, by the bed. HARPO points the hooter at BRIGGS as he turns. BRIGGS thinks it's a gun and puts up his hands. HARPO slaps hands with him and BRIGGS knocks him over on the bed.

Resume on HELTON as BRIGGS comes up to him.

44

Briggs furious: *So you got your gang with you, hey? Well, I'll get you later.* He goes off.

By the bed, Chico and Harpo return to their game while Briggs slams out of the door in the background. Helton appears and stands over them.

Helton: *Who are you guys?* They signal to him to keep quiet. *What are you doing in my room?*

Chico: *'At'sa my partner, but he no speak. He'sa dem an a-duff.*

Helton picks up the hooter from the bed and Harpo squeezes the bulb. Sound of the hooter.

Helton laughing: *You guys don't know it, but you just scared a pretty tough egg out of this room.*

Chico: *Sure, we're a couple tough guys.*

Helton leans forward, in medium close-up.

Helton: *Do you wanna make some money?*

Resume on the three of them. Chico and Harpo are on their feet and standing beside him almost before he has got out the words. They rub their hands with glee.

Chico: *Money?* He chuckles. *Money, hey? Feela this mos'le.*

45

HELTON does so. *Feela his mos'le.*

HARPO gives him his leg. HELTON laughs and squeezes it; HARPO winces.

CHICO : *All right, all right. How much you pay?*

A closer shot of the three of them.

HELTON : *Well, just how tough are you?*

CHICO : *Well, you pay little bit, we little bit tough. You pay very much, very much tough. You pay too much, we too much tough. How much you pay?*

HELTON : *I pay plenty.*

CHICO : *Well, then we're plenty tough. And we show you, too.*

He pushes HELTON off and beckons to HARPO.

CHICO : *Hey, partner, show 'im how tough we are.*

HARPO rolls up his sleeve and hits CHICO on the jaw.

CHICO turning to HELTON : *See? 'At'sa nothing, 'at'sa free.*

HELTON is seen from a low angle, watching sceptically.

CHICO off : *Now, we give you da real stuff this time.*

Resume on the other two.

CHICO to HARPO : *Hey, come on, put some pep into it. The one-two upper-cut. You know, on the button.*

HARPO takes aim at his navel.

CHICO : *No, no — no downstairs button, upstairs button.*

HARPO cracks him on the jaw . . .

CHICO flies through the air . . .

And lands on his back on the floor.

HELTON stands watching. He looks from CHICO to HARPO and grins.

Resume on HARPO : he grins back at HELTON, teeth bared.

CHICO gets up in front of him.

CHICO pushing him around : *'At'sa fine, hey? 'At's good, all right. I tell him you're tough and you punch like a lily. What'sa matter with you. You wanna lose-a this job? Give 'im the stuff this time.*

Camera pans with CHICO as he goes across to HELTON.

CHICO : *Excusa me, boss, he canna do much better, but he no work good today. You see, he'sa no getta paid. But when he getta paid, you watch him.*

We follow him back to HARPO again.

CHICO : *Come on. This time we give 'im the works. Come on, hurry up. On the button this time.* He pushes him, egging him on.

46

Come on. I tell you, on the button. Come on, hurry. Come on. Give him da punch.

HARPO clenches his fists and starts to pant, rolling his eyes and baring his teeth.

CHICO urgently : *Come on, come on, come on. All right, all right.*

Close-up of HARPO, panting and glaring.

CHICO off : *Come on. Punch! Punch!*

HARPO swings at CHICO.

In a general shot of the scene, he cracks him on the jaw again. CHICO flies through the air, lands on the bed . . .

And somersaults on to the floor, seen from a high angle.

Resume on HARPO, still panting and glaring. Suddenly the frog croaks inside his hat and the crown moves up and down. HARPO looks up and grins.

Laid out on the floor beside the bed, CHICO starts to come to . . . While HARPO starts glaring again and runs forward.

Back to the scene. HELTON comes across and helps CHICO to his feet, while HARPO grabs the hooter from the bed and takes a swing at him.

CHICO restraining HARPO : *Hey, 'at'sa nuf. Wait.* To HELTON : *Well, what you think of us?*

HELTON : *You're great.*

CHICO : *Sssh! Not so loud. You want him to getta swell head?*

HELTON : *You guys are plenty tough all right.*

He turns and opens a closet beside the bed.

At that moment GROUCHO, in close-up, pokes his head through the window and calls out :

GROUCHO : *I'm spying on you!*

Shot of HARPO and CHICO. CHICO shushes GROUCHO, off; HARPO shushes CHICO.

Back to the scene as HELTON comes up to the two of them again.

HELTON : *You're just the fellows I need. You're hired.*

He exits into the closet, taking off his dressing gown. CHICO holds out his hand to shake with HARPO; HARPO gives him the bulb of the hooter; the hooter sounds and CHICO runs into the closet.

CHICO comes up to HELTON inside the closet. As they talk, HELTON takes off his dressing gown and reaches for a jacket.

47

CHICO : *Hey, we're great, huh?*
HELTON : *You're great.*
CHICO : *Sure, my partner's great.*
HELTON : *He's great.*
CHICO : *My grandfather's great. He a great-grandfather.*
> On the deck outside, BRIGGS, GROUCHO and ZEPPO emerge from behind a companion way and look off.
BRIGGS : *Now when he comes out, plug him.*
ZEPPO : *Yeah? What'll we plug him with?*
BRIGGS : *Didn't I give you two gats?*
GROUCHO : *Well, we had to drown the gats, but we saved you a little black gitten.*
> BRIGGS pulls out two more guns.
BRIGGS : *Here, take these, and hang onto 'em now.*
> He gives them the guns and they look at them nervously.
> Inside the stateroom, HELTON gives a gun each to HARPO and CHICO.
HELTON : *Don't leave me for a minute. And keep your eyes on that guy that just went out of here.* He goes off to the closet again.
CHICO to HARPO : *Now, you understand? Anybody comes near da boss, let 'im have it.*
> He slaps his hand with the gun butt. HELTON reappears, putting on a cloth cap. CHICO steps up to him.
CHICO : *You're all right now, boss. Anybody comes near you . . .*
> HARPO hits him on the head with the gun butt.
CHICO : *Hey, what'sa matter with you? Look out.* To HELTON : *That's all right, he was just practising.*
> He mutters at HARPO who gives him his leg; CHICO thrusts him aside.
HELTON : *Now I can take a walk out on deck and feel safe. Come on, let's go.*
> In a closer shot, the three of them pass by the bed and go towards the door, HARPO brandishing his hooter.
> As they are about to leave, HARPO dodges back to the chessboard, makes a final move and returns to the door, putting a piece in his pocket.
> Out on the deck, BRIGGS, GROUCHO and ZEPPO are seen by the companion way, looking off.
BRIGGS : *There he comes now. Get him.* He goes off.

GROUCHO : *Don't worry, we'll get him. I've got my finger on the trigger.*

He unconsciously points his gun at ZEPPO's stomach and ZEPPO dodges back nervously.

HELTON now appears in a doorway, flanked by HARPO and CHICO with their guns. He looks round warily and exits to the left, while the other two peer behind them. Simultaneously GIBSON appears, going towards the right, and HARPO and CHICO follow him off, unaware, searching to and fro for potential enemies. HARPO holds his gun butt-forwards.

In a long shot of the promenade deck, GIBSON strides towards us with HARPO and CHICO prowling behind, guns at the ready, There is a buzz of voices as the passengers leap up in alarm.

Camera tracks ahead of HARPO and CHICO as they walk along. CHICO : *Hey, don't forget, anybody comes near the boss, let 'im have it.*

Resume on all three of them as GIBSON arrives at the bottom of a stairway and looks up it, then goes off in the opposite direction. HARPO tries to follow a couple of passing girls, but

CHICO hauls him back and they follow a passenger in a white cap as he mounts the stairs.

At the top of the stairs, two passengers hurry off in alarm as the man comes into view, followed by CHICO and HARPO. We move with them past a row of deck chairs; a woman jumps up with a scream.

We now see the trio coming along the boat deck towards us. HARPO and CHICO turn round, grinning at the frightened passengers. In so doing, they lose the man in the white hat and start following a passenger with a beard, who gets up from a deck chair just in front of them.

The man moves away from camera, then stops and turns. HARPO and CHICO stand amazed as they see his face, then CHICO bursts out laughing.

A closer shot of the three of them

CHICO pointing : *Hey, it's da boss. He's gotta disguise. Take off the whiskers, we know ya.*

HARPO puts his knee against the man's chest and tugs at the beard.

Man indignant: *Ouch! What do you mean?* Waving: *Officer! Officer!*

Resume on the previous shot as Harpo and Chico exit in opposite directions.

Man: *Officer!*

Gibson passes at a run.

On another part of the boat deck, Briggs appears in the foreground and signals to Groucho and Zeppo. They hurry up and stand on either side of him.

Briggs: *Well, why didn't you get him? Not afraid, are you?*

Zeppo: *Well, we were ...*

Groucho: *Afraid? Me? A man who's licked his weight in wild caterpillars? Afraid! ... You bet I'm afraid.*

Lucille comes up behind them, furious.

Lucille: *So ...!*

Groucho: *Hello. How are things in the closet? You know, I still smell of moth balls.*

Lucille standing nose to nose with him: *Oh, I don't want to talk to you.*

She stamps her foot and turns away. Groucho grabs her from

behind and sweeps her into a tango, humming. They circle round the deck.

In a reverse shot they return to the other two. GROUCHO does a final pirouette.

LUCILLE to BRIGGS : *So, here you are, loafing around with these tramps!*

BRIGGS : *I tell you, I came down to see Joe Helton.*

ZEPPO to GROUCHO : *Don't you think we'd better go?*

GROUCHO : *What, and leave this woman alone with her husband? Suppose her sweetheart came in?*

LUCILLE poking BRIGGS in the chest : *Let me tell you, Alky Briggs, don't think you can keep me cooped up in that stateroom below, because you're crazy.*

ZEPPO leans back against the wall, while GROUCHO stands between BRIGGS and LUCILLE, listening.

BRIGGS : *You're going to stay down there like I told you and keep out of my business, do you understand? Keep out of my business.*

Medium close-up of BRIGGS, GROUCHO and LUCILLE.

LUCILLE : *Oh, you were going to show me a good time. A good time! Well, I might as well have stayed at home and played solitaire.*

GROUCHO to BRIGGS : *Your turn.*

BRIGGS : *Pipe down, will ya? I have more important things to worry about.*

GROUCHO to LUCILLE : *Your turn.*

LUCILLE advancing on BRIGGS : *You say that to me again and I'll scratch your eyes out.*

GROUCHO : *Here, big boy, you take this gun. You're going to need it more than I will.*

He hands BRIGGS his gun and steps between them.

Shot of the scene as GROUCHO and ZEPPO exit on the left.

LUCILLE : *Oh, you . . .!*

She exits to the right, followed by BRIGGS.

In the main salon, HARPO chases the chambermaid down the stairs and round the fountain at the bottom. He passes a female the stairs.

On the boat deck, HELTON is sitting back in a deck chair,

53

reading a magazine. GROUCHO strides up and slaps him on the foot.

GROUCHO standing over him : *You're just the man I want to see. If I could show you how to save twenty per cent, would you be interested? Of course you would . . . In the first place, your overhead is too high and your brow is too low. Interested already, aren't you?*

HELTON : *I . . .*

A closer shot of both.

GROUCHO raising a hand : *Now, just wait till I get through.*

HELTON : *I haven't got time.*

GROUCHO : *Now, there are two fellas trying to attack you, aren't there? And there are two fellas trying to defend you.*

HELTON : *Why . . .*

GROUCHO : *Now that's fifty per cent waste. Now why can't you be attacked by your own bodyguards? Your life will be saved, and that's . . . that's a hundred per cent waste.*

HELTON stares at him, bewildered.

GROUCHO : *Now what have you got? You've still got me and I'll attack you for nothing.*

HELTON : *Say, what are you getting at?*

GROUCHO : *I anticipated that question. How does an army travel? On its stomach. How do you travel? On a ship.* Waving his cigar : *Of course, you're saving your stomach. Now, that same common sense will . . .*

HELTON : *I don't think you realize . . .*

GROUCHO : *Oh I realize it's a penny here and a penny there, but look at me. I've worked myself up from nothing to a state of extreme poverty. Now what do you say?*

HELTON : *I'll tell you what I say. I say . . .*

The two of them are seen in medium close-up.

GROUCHO : *All right. Then it's settled. I'm to be your new bodyguard. In case I'm gonna attack you, I'll have to be there to defend you, too.*

HELTON springs to his feet.

GROUCHO : *Now, let me know when you want to be attacked, and I'll be there ten minutes later to defend you.*

HELTON : *I've already got two bodyguards, but I'll think it over.*

We cut to the corridor outside the barber's shop, where HARPO is strolling to and fro, whistling. He suddenly slips on the polished floor, losing his hat, and the frog escapes.

Seen from above, it leaps away across the floor.

Inside the barber's shop, a customer is just putting on his jacket as HARPO enters in search of the frog, whistling. The man tips the BARBER.

BARBER : *Thank you.*

MAN croaking : *You're welcome.*

BARBER : *Why, what's the matter with you?*

MAN croaking : *I've got a frog in my throat.*

A closer shot of the two of them as HARPO, who is searching round in the background, turns to listen.

BARBER : *What?*

MAN croaking : *A frog — a frog in my throat.*

BARBER loudly : *Oh, you've got a frog in your throat.*

MAN croaking : *Yes.*

HARPO grabs the man and wrenches open his jaw, looking down his throat.

Resume on the scene as he turns the man upside down, shaking him.

BARBER : *Hey! You can't do that to my customers. Cut it out. Say, what's the matter with you? Are you crazy or something?*

At that moment the frog croaks off-screen and we cut back to the previous shot as HARPO looks round wildly, clapping his hand over the man's mouth.

Back to the scene. Camera pans as HARPO thrusts the man aside, grabs his hat and hooter, and runs to the door, whistling. We see the frog on the floor of the corridor outside. HARPO appears in the foreground and kneels down, whistling and beckoning. The frog jumps into the hat and HARPO gets up, scolding it. It croaks in reply and he puts on his hat, looking relieved. Fade out.

On the sound of the ship's siren, we fade in to the New York shoreline in the distance.

General shot of the deck. The passengers are sitting or standing around with their luggage. GIBSON steps forward and calls out :

GIBSON : *Have your landing cards and passports ready, please.*

On another part of the deck, a tall, opulently dressed middle-aged woman comes and stands by some luggage; a couple of reporters step up to her.

FIRST REPORTER : *How do you do, Madame Swempski?*

MADAME SWEMPSKI : *Oh, hello boys.*

A closer shot of the three of them.

FIRST REPORTER : *Any statement for the press this time?*

MADAME SWEMPSKI affably : *No, I'm afraid not. Nothing of interest on this last tour.*

FIRST REPORTER : *Is it true that the opera is on the decline in Central Europe, Madame?*

MADAME SWEMPSKI : *Absurd. I predict they're going to have the greatest year they've ever had in grand opera.*

They write in their notebooks, as GROUCHO comes up and stands on the luggage behind them, looking over their shoulders.

SECOND REPORTER : *Pardon me, is it true that you're going to get married again while on this tour?*

MADAME SWEMPSKI coyly : *Why, gentlemen.* She laughs . . . *I . . . I don't know what to say . . .*

Groucho steps down between her and the reporters.

Groucho waving his cigar: *Gentlemen, I'd say just this. The bicycle will never replace the horse. On the other hand the horse will never replace the bicycle . . .*

Madame Swempski looks indignant.

Groucho: *. . . which is quite a horse on the bicycle if I ever saw one, and I don't think I ever saw one.* He snaps his fingers at the reporters. *I dare you to print that, you muck-rakers! Have a cigar, babe?*

He takes a cigar from his breast pocket and offers it to Madame Swempski.

First Reporter to a photographer, off-screen: *Okay for the picture, Joe.*

Shot of the scene as Groucho sits down on the luggage and pulls up his trouser leg.

Groucho: *Pictures? Here's a little sex stuff for your front page.*

We see the photographer standing by his camera, which is on a tripod with a black cloth over it.

Photographer: *Now hold it steady, please.*

He presses the bulb; it makes a noise like a hooter.

Cut to a closer shot as he whips off the cover in amazement, revealing Harpo standing underneath. Harpo exits, scattering the tripod legs.

We return to the other four.

Groucho getting up: *And you can see it was a real love match. We married for money . . .*

He puts his arm round Madame Swempski, in medium close-up.

Groucho: *Eh, my shrinking violet?* Prodding her: *Say, it wouldn't hurt you to shrink thirty or forty pounds.*

Madame Swempski: *Oh, you impudent cad! I'll report you to your paper.*

Back to the four of them.

Groucho: *I'll thank you to let me do the reporting.* He grabs the first reporter's notebook. *Is it true you're getting a divorce as soon as your husband recovers his eyesight? Is it true that you wash your hair in clam broth? Is it true you used to dance in a flee circus?*

Madame Swempski indignantly: *This is outrageous! If you don't*

57

stop, I'll call the Captain.

GROUCHO : *Oh, so that's it. Infatuated with a pretty uniform!* Gesturing to the reporters : *We don't count, after we've given you the best years of our lives. You have to have an officer.* He hands back the notebook.

MADAME SWEMPSKI : *I don't like this innuendo.*

GROUCHO : *That's what I always say. Love flies out the door when money comes innuendo. Well, goodbye.* He picks up a suitcase and shakes her hand. *It's nice to have seen you, but I've got nobody to blame but myself. Ta-ta.*

Shot of the scene as GROUCHO goes off, camera panning with him.

REPORTER off : *Now, could you tell me . . .*

MADAME SWEMPSKI in a tired voice, off : *Oh, please . . .*

Music as we move to a shot of ZEPPO and MARY, sitting side by side.

MARY : *You're awfully glum.*

ZEPPO taking her hand : *I was just thinking, after the boat lands I may never see you again.*

MARY : *Does it matter to you whether you ever see me again?*

ZEPPO : *I can't think of anything in the world that matters more. Mary, I'll never leave you.*

Sound of running feet, off. ZEPPO leaps up, and we cut to a longer shot as he exits, pursued by GIBSON.

Shot of the passengers standing amid their luggage, waiting to get off the boat. A steward is squatting on the floor, handing out luggage tags as GROUCHO, HARPO and CHICO come up. They each grab a bag and hurry past.

STEWARD to each of them in turn : *Tag. Tag. Tag.* HARPO doesn't take his . . . *Tag.*

HARPO tags the steward and runs off.

We are now looking onto the boat from the top of the gangway, with an officer standing on each side. HARPO, CHICO and GROUCHO hurry forward with their bags, but the officers hold them back.

OFFICER : *Wait a minute. Wait a minute.*

GROUCHO : *Well, I'm just trying to sneak off the boat, that's all.*

CHICO : *I'm lookin' for the man who owns this grip.*

ZEPPO comes up behind them.

58

OFFICER : *Where's your passport?*

They back off and go into a huddle.

GROUCHO : *Wait a minute. Wait a minute. Let me handle this.*

He goes up to the officer on the right, and we cut to a shot of the two of them.

GROUCHO : *Ahem! I don't like to speak about it, officer, but I happen to be a good friend of the man who supplies the meat for this boat.*

OFFICER unimpressed : *Well?*

GROUCHO : *Well, do you like lamb chops?*

OFFICER : *Yes. What of it?*

GROUCHO : *Well, this man doesn't handle any lamb chops, but the roast beef is very good today.*

Resume on the scene from the top of the gangway.

OFFICER : *Say, now listen, you fellas can't get off the boat without showing passports.*

There is more shouting and arguing as they are pushed away from the gangway. HARPO swings from the second officer's arm.

OFFICER : *Go on, get back.*

We move to a shot of the swing doors near the top of the gangway; camera pans with the Marx brothers as they come through and ZEPPO goes off.

GROUCHO : *Stuffed shirt! You know, when he said that to me, you could have knocked me over with a feather.*

HARPO takes a feather from his pocket and hits GROUCHO over the head; GROUCHO falls in CHICO's arms.

CHICO : *He gives you service.*

Seen in close-up, HARPO takes an iron bar from inside the feather and drops it.

It lands with a crash on the floor.

Then we resume on the three of them.

GROUCHO : *Well, it looks like we're up against it.* To HARPO : *It's up to you to get us a passport.*

A man goes past towards the swing doors. HARPO follows and puts a hand in the man's pocket. The man stops and grabs him by the wrist.

MAN : *I got you, didn't I! Well, you'll have to get up pretty early in the morning to steal from me.*

GROUCHO : *He did get up early this morning, but you weren't here.*

Could he see you some time tomorrow?
MAN : *Aww!*
He lets go of HARPO and exits through the swing doors.
GROUCHO : *Well, come on, let's try another one, huh?*
Another man passes. CHICO follows and puts a hand in his pocket. The man turns and grabs him by the wrist.
MAN : *What's the idea, putting your hand in my pocket?*
CHICO : *Just a little mistake. I had a suit once looked just like that, and for a moment I thought those were my pants.*
MAN : *How could they be your pants when I've got them on?*
CHICO : *Well, this suit had two pair of pants.*
MAN releasing him : *You'd better keep your hands to yourself.*
Shot of the group as the man exits through the swing doors and ZEPPO enters from the right.
ZEPPO : *Do you know who's on this boat?*
GROUCHO : *No.*
ZEPPO : *Maurice Chevalier, the movie actor. I just ran into him.*
GROUCHO : *Did you hurt him?*
CHICO : *How did you know it was Chevalier?*
ZEPPO pulls out a passport.
ZEPPO : *I got his passport. Right here.*
A closer shot of the four of them as they pass it round.
GROUCHO : *Now he can't get off the boat.*
HARPO grabs the passport, looks at the photograph and grimaces, thrusting out his lower lip.
CHICO : *Hey, he looks like Chevalier.*
GROUCHO : *Yes, that's true.*
CHICO grimacing : *And I can talk like Chevalier.*
GROUCHO grimacing : *And I certainly look like Chevalier.*
Camera pans towards ZEPPO.
ZEPPO : *But that's not enough. You've gotta sing one of Chevalier's songs to get off this boat.*
He sings, with his hand on his heart :
ZEPPO : ' *If the nightingales*
Could sing like you,
They'd sing much better
Than you do . . .'
GROUCHO : *That's dandy. If you sing like that, they'll put us all off the boat.*

Resume on the scene.

CHICO : *Well, let's try it.*

GROUCHO : *All right. Come on, come on. Let's go.*

They all hurry off.

The scene moves to the passport control in the main saloon. The passengers are queuing at a long table with several passport officers at its head, one of them standing and calling out instructions.

OFFICER : *Have your passports ready.* To a passenger : *Right straight up, you'll find the baggage on the deck.* Inspecting another's passport : *Okay . . . Have your passports ready. Keep in line, everybody. Nine forty-five. Keep in line, everybody. Have your passports ready.*

A closer shot of the passengers queuing at the table as the four Marx brothers come up in the background, all wearing straw boaters except for HARPO. Camera pans with them as they crawl under the table and along on the opposite side to the queue. HARPO tries to ride on GROUCHO's back.

We now see the end of the table as the Marx brothers crawl

61

back under it and come up at the head of the queue.

OFFICER : *Ten ninety-two . . .*

Another shot of the head of the table, with the passport officers seated in back view as the Marx brothers surface on the other side. HARPO grabs a rubber stamp and starts stamping everything in sight. General shouts and confusion.

PASSPORT OFFICERS : *Hey! Hey! Hey!*

The standing OFFICER addresses them.

OFFICER : *Hey, if you want to get off the boat, get in the back.*

GROUCHO swapping hats with him : *Oh, I didn't get on in the back. I got on in the front.*

OFFICER swapping the hats back : *Never mind where you got on.*

GROUCHO, HARPO and CHICO leave, shoved by the OFFICER.

ZEPPO : *You're perfectly right, officer. I told those fellows to stay in line.*

OFFICER : *Yeah? Well, let me see your passport.*

ZEPPO : *Yeah, right here.*

They are seen in medium close-up as ZEPPO hands over the passport.

ZEPPO pointing : *That's my name.*

OFFICER sceptically : *Maurice Chevalier, eh?*

ZEPPO : *Yeah.*

OFFICER : *Say, this picture doesn't look like you.*

ZEPPO : *Sure I'm Maurice Chevalier. I'll sing for you.*

Music. We cut to a medium shot as ZEPPO does his Chevalier routine, dancing and waving his boater.

ZEPPO singing : ' *If a nightingale*
Could sing like you,
They'd sing much better
Than they do . . .'

He tries to dance past the OFFICER, but the latter grabs him.

OFFICER : *Here. Never mind this! Get back in line where you belong!* He shoves him to the back of the queue.

Resume on the other end of the table as CHICO now runs up with the passport, followed by GROUCHO. Camera moves with them as they push their way to the head of the table, where CHICO engages the standing OFFICER, while GROUCHO turns to the indignant MADAME SWEMPSKI just behind him.

OFFICER to CHICO : *Let me have your passport. Say, this picture doesn't look like you.*

CHICO: *I know it don't look like me from the front, but you go in the back of the boat — it just like me.*

OFFICER: *You're not Maurice Chevalier.*

CHICO: *Are you Maurice Chevalier?*

OFFICER: *No.*

CHICO: *Well, there you are. Wait, I prove it.*

Music; he sings, waving his boater.

CHICO: ' *If a nightingale*
    Could sing like you,
    He sing much better
    Than you do,
    And . . .'

The OFFICER grabs him and shoves him to the back.

OFFICER: *Hey! Out! Out!*

CHICO: *Hey! No pusha me!*

OFFICER: *Get out of here! Get back in line where you belong!*

CHICO leaves, handing the passport to GROUCHO, who steps up to the OFFICER.

OFFICER: *Passport!*

GROUCHO hands it over, tilting his boater to hide his face.

OFFICER: *Say, this picture doesn't look like you.*

GROUCHO: *Well, it doesn't look like you either.*

OFFICER: *This man has no moustache.*

GROUCHO: *Well, the barber shop wasn't open this morning.*

OFFICER: *Why, look at that face.*

GROUCHO pointing to MADAME SWEMPSKI: *Well, look at that face.*

MADAME SWEMPSKI: *Ohhh!*

GROUCHO pointing back at the OFFICER: *All right, look at that face.*

OFFICER: *Hey, are you going to identify yourself, or else . . .*

Music. GROUCHO sings, waving his boater.

GROUCHO: ' *If a nightingale*
    Could sing like you,
    They'd sing much better
    Than they do,
    You brought a new kind of love
    To me . . .'

The OFFICER grabs him and shoves him to the back.

OFFICER: *Outside! Back in line where you belong.*

Groucho leaves.

Resume on the other end of the table. Camera pans with Harpo as he climbs onto it and strolls along the top with his hooter, nodding to the indignant passengers.

We see him again as he arrives at the head of the table and stands over the passport officers amid their papers. General confusion.

Passport Officers shouting: *Get off that table! What do you think ... Get him off that table anyway!*

Harpo works a date stamp with his foot; the standing Officer yells at him.

Officer: *Come off there!*

Harpo jumps down and starts throwing papers in the air. The Officer grabs him round the waist.

Officer: *Lunatic!*

Harpo carries on throwing papers, jiggles the pens in the pen holder and drums his hands on the table in maniac glee.

A closer shot of him and the Officer.

Officer beside himself: *Passport!* Harpo produces a piece of pasteboard. *I said passport ...*

Resume on the scene.

Officer throwing it down: *... not pasteboard!* Harpo offers his leg. *Come on with that passport.*

Harpo produces a washboard. The Officer throws it down.

Officer: *Not washboard.* Beating his fist on the table: *Passport!*

Harpo finally produces the passport, stamps it and hands it to the Officer.

Close-up of the passport with Chevalier's photograph.

Officer practically speechless, off: *Chevalier ... eh?*

Resume on the two of them. Harpo restrains the Officer and starts miming to a record of the Chevalier song.

Chevalier's Voice: '*If a nightingale*
Could sing like you,
They'd sing much sweeter
Than they do,
For you brought a new kind of love
To me.
If the sandman ...'

The record runs down and Harpo turns to reveal a gramophone strapped to his back, which he winds furiously. The record picks up again.

CHEVALIER'S VOICE: '... *To live my whole life through,*
For you brought a new kind of love
To me ...'

Shot of the scene as the OFFICER grabs HARPO, losing his cap. HARPO goes wild, stamping everything in sight — the papers, the table, the OFFICER's bald head — while everyone tries to restrain him.

PASSPORT OFFICERS shouting: *Get him out of here! Put him back! Put him back where he belongs!*

The OFFICER finally ejects him.

On the deck, GIBSON is standing by the swing doors leading out to the gangplank, a stream of passengers moving slowly towards him. A fat man in a straw boater hurries into view.

GIBSON: *Take it easy, folks. The gangplank is to the left, please. Don't crowd.*

In a closer shot the camera pans with the FAT MAN as he pushes his way to the head of the queue.

GIBSON: *Don't crowd.*

The FAT MAN reaches GIBSON, almost knocking over MADAME SWEMPSKI.

GIBSON: *Take your time. Ladies first.*

FAT MAN: *Let me off the boat. I'm a sick man. I feel faint.*

GIBSON: *I don't care. Take your time.*

FAT MAN frantically, mopping his face: *I tell you I feel faint. I'm going ... I'm going to faint.*

He collapses into GIBSON's arms.

MADAME SWEMPSKI: *Oh! Oh, someone get a doctor!*

Back to the scene as she hurries along the corridor towards us, then cut to a closer shot, camera panning as she hurries along.

MADAME SWEMPSKI: *Where's a doctor? A doctor! I want a doctor!*

She encounters HARPO and CHICO who grab her and lay her in a deck chair.

CHICO: *She'sa sick. All right, all right, we take care of you ...* She drums her feet, speechless ... *Look, she's gotta chill. Cover her up. Cover her up.*

65

Harpo sits on top of her.

Madame Swempski in a muffled voice: *Oh! Oh! Oh!*

Chico: *Oh, no, no, no. Get up, get up! Take her pulse!*

A closer shot of the three of them. Harpo grabs her purse and pockets it.

Chico: *Take her pulse. No purse — put it back* . . . Harpo does so . . . *Pulse.*

Madame Swempski struggles wildly, but Chico holds her down, as he says to Harpo:

Chico: *I think you best take the temperature. That's good. All right, we take care of you, lady.*

Harpo pulls out a pipe, shakes it and thrusts it into her mouth.

Chico: *All right, all right, all right, all right.*

Resume on the scene as she finally springs up and throws down the pipe.

Madame Swempski: *Oh, you fools! I'm not the patient!*

Chico hands her her fur coat.

Chico: *Well, we're not the doctor* . . . *Come on.* He leads Harpo off.

On another part of the deck, a middle-aged passenger is sitting asleep, wearing dark glasses. Other passengers pass to and fro in front of him, then a man in a white cap hurries into view.

Man: *Doctor! Doctor! Is there a doctor on the boat? Doctor!*

He goes off; Groucho appears from the right; a second man enters.

Second Man: *Doctor! Doctor!* To Groucho: *Are you a doctor?*

Groucho: *Sure, I'm a doctor. Where's the horse?*

Second Man pointing: *Why, a man fainted over here.*

Groucho: *Man fainted? I'll soon fix that* . . .

The man goes off; Groucho grabs the dark glasses from the sleeping passenger and lopes after him.

Groucho: *Just my hard luck it couldn't be a woman!*

Camera pans with Groucho as he runs along the corridor, grabbing a black bag from a pile of luggage as he passes. He reaches a group of passengers gathered round the fainted man. Gibson is bent over him, while another man fans him with his hat. Groucho grabs one of the standing passengers by the wrist and takes his pulse.

Groucho: *Hmmm. Just as I thought — smoking too much.*

66

GIBSON on his knees: *Here he is here, doctor.*
GROUCHO: *Don't tell me, I'll find him myself.*
In a closer shot, GROUCHO kneels down beside the man and pulls out a stethoscope. He puts it in the man's ears and listens at the wrong end, then gets up again.
GROUCHO: *I can't do anything for that man. He's fainted.* He pulls out a pad and writes a prescription. *In the meantime, get him off the boat and have his baggage examined.*
He hands the prescription to GIBSON off-screen.
A MAN off: *Gangway!*
GROUCHO beckoning to the passengers: *Will you all get close so he won't recover? Here, right this way.*
Shot of the scene as everyone closes in around the man.
GROUCHO: *Step right around here.*
He steps over the man's body and makes off.
On the other side of the swing doors, some sailors carry a covered stretcher out towards the gangway.
GIBSON is seen in back view at the top of the gangway.
GIBSON: *Step lively down there.*
The sailors carry the stretcher down the gangplank and GIBSON follows them part of the way down.
A high angle shot shows the scene at the bottom of the gangway, as the sailors lay down the stretcher on the quay.
SAILOR: *Hey, back that ambulance in here.*
The sailors go off. GROUCHO, HARPO, CHICO and ZEPPO throw the cover aside and rise from the stretcher. General laughter. GROUCHO waves up to GIBSON.
We see GIBSON from below on the gangway.
GIBSON: *Hey!*
Resume on the quayside; the Marx brothers stand in a row grinning up at him.
GIBSON off: *Hey!*

The scene dissolves to an insert of a newspaper headline which reads: BIG JOE HELTON HOME FROM ABROAD PLANS ELABORATE PARTY TO INTRODUCE DAUGHTER.
Dissolve again to a poorly furnished room, where BRIGGS is standing over two of his gang — BUTCH and SHORTY — who

67

are seated at a table. SHORTY is holding a saxophone; another man, SPIKE, is seen reflected in a mirror.

BRIGGS : *Helton's throwing his party tonight, and this time we'll blow the works. Now you guys are going in as musicians, and stay that way until I give you the office.*

SPIKE : *Say, what about those four guys in the house, the ones that you said were on the bat?*

BRIGGS : *Aw, don't worry about them. They eat out of my hand.*

SPIKE comes up to them, holding a bottle of milk.

BRIGGS : *The main thing for you to worry about is that girl. Keep an eye on her. Get me?* He lights a cigarette.

SPIKE : *That ought to be easy to take.*

He picks up a sandwich from the table and drinks from the milk bottle.

BRIGGS : *Okay. Sit tight and I'll give you a call.*

He moves off. Fade out.

Fade in to the exterior of JOE HELTON's palatial residence. It is night; light floods from the windows and gay music is heard. A large limousine drives up to the front steps and several people in party clothes get out.

Dissolve to the interior of the house; in the drawing room a band is playing and couples are dancing, seen from above.

A closer shot of the dancers; most of them are in fancy dress. Outside, another car full of guests draws up, with CHICO and HARPO riding on the off-side running board. The guests get out, while HARPO and CHICO clamber into the car, leave again from the near-side and follow them up the steps. The car drives off. As HARPO and CHICO reach the top of the steps, the door is slammed in their faces.

A closer shot shows HARPO and CHICO peering in through the glass door. It opens and two thugs in evening dress come out.

MAN threatening : *Say, have you guys got an invitation?*

CHICO : *We give you invitation of Chevalier.*

He sings, while HARPO whistles in accompaniment.

CHICO : *' When the nightingale*
    Sing like you,
    He sing much . . .'

MAN : *Hey! Cut it out! And stay away from this door, see?*

He goes in and slams the door.

We return to the drawing room, where ZEPPO appears in back view, peering around amongst the guests.

He is seen again standing by an open doorway leading out into the hall. MARY comes down the staircase in the background and he calls up to her.

ZEPPO : *Mary!*

Camera tracks forward into the hall as he meets her at the bottom of the stairs and takes her by the hand.

ZEPPO : *You certainly had me worried. I thought you'd forgotten your own party.*

Track out again as they advance to the door of the drawing room.

MARY : *You haven't been doing all the worrying. I was afraid you wouldn't come.*

BUTCH, SHORTY and SPIKE are seen playing in the band. SHORTY nudges BUTCH.

The couple dance away from the drawing room door . . .

And the three thugs follow them with their eyes.

We see the couple in medium close-up, dancing.

MARY looking round : *My, but there're a lot of strange-looking people here.*

On the other side of the room, camera moves with GROUCHO as he lopes past the band and in amongst the dancing couples. He climbs onto a couch at the end of the room and calls for silence.

GROUCHO : *Ladies and gentlemen!* The music stops. *Quiet, everybody, quiet!*

A closer shot of him.

GROUCHO : *A lady's diamond earring has been lost. It looks exactly like this.* He holds up an earring. *In fact, this is it.*

Resume on the scene as he vaults over a balustrade behind the couch, then cut to reverse shot as he lands beside a tall woman sitting on another couch on the other side.

WOMAN haughtily : *I beg your pardon!*

GROUCHO : *How about you and I passing out on the veranda, or would you rather pass out here?*

He grabs her by the hand and pulls her to her feet.

WOMAN looking down her nose : *Sir, you have the advantage of me!*

70

(She is a good head taller than he is.)

GROUCHO rolling his eyes : *Not yet I haven't, but wait till I get you outside.*

He grabs her; she pushes him away.

WOMAN : *You're pretty fresh, aren't you?*

GROUCHO starts to take off his jacket.

Shot of the scene as a man in Indian costume comes up and grabs GROUCHO by the shoulder.

MAN : *Hey, that's my wife and I don't like the way you're acting around here.*

GROUCHO : *Well, if you don't like our country, why don't you go back where you came from.*

The man brandishes his tomahawk.

MAN : *Say, I ought to sink that right in your scalp.*

He takes a swing at GROUCHO, but is restrained by his wife.

GROUCHO dodges past her and taps a fat man standing nearby on the back.

GROUCHO : *Run for your life. The Indians are coming!*

FAT MAN turning in alarm : *What?*

GROUCHO : *Put your scalp in your pocket.* He takes off the man's

toupée and hands it to him. *Here. The Indians.*
FAT MAN : *Oh!*

GROUCHO exits with a warwhoop. The husband starts after him and bumps into the fat man.

MAN waving his tomahawk : *I'll get him!*

Out in the hall, HELTON is welcoming a couple of guests as GROUCHO comes out doing an Indian dance and whooping. The guests go into the drawing room. HELTON slaps GROUCHO on the back.

HELTON : *Have a good time, kid.*

A closer shot of the two of them.

HELTON : *This is gonna be a real party.*

GROUCHO : *You call this a party? The beer is warm, the women are cold and I'm hot under the collar . . . In fact, a more poisonous little barbecue I've never attended.*

HELTON : *Say, you're a funny kind of a duck, but I like you. You stick by me, and I'll stick by you.*

GROUCHO claps him on the shoulder, clasps his hand and addresses him in a Texan drawl.

73

GROUCHO : *Sheriff, I ain't much on flowery sentiments, but there's somethin' I jes' got to tell yuh . . . Shucks, man, I'd be nuthin' but a pizenous varmint and not fitten to touch the hem of yo' pants if I didn't tell you you've treated me squar, mighty squar, and I ain't fergettin' it.*

With bowed legs, he walks into the drawing room, past a couple standing in the doorway, the man wearing a cowboy outfit. Then he comes back towards HELTON, grabbing the man's ten-gallon hat as he passes.

GROUCHO : *Sheriff, I ain't fergettin'.*

He goes off in the foreground with legs bowed, wearing the hat. Sound of a horse neighing.

GROUCHO off : *Whoa theah, Bessie, whoa theah.*

Hoofbeats. HELTON and his guests burst out laughing.

We move to the interior of the drawing room as a large floral decoration is carried in. HELTON enters and stands in front of it. Applause.

HELTON : *My friends, this is indeed a surprise . . .*

He beckons, and MARY appears followed by ZEPPO.

HELTON : *. . . You couldn't have pleased me better.*

A closer shot of HELTON and MARY.

HELTON : *And now I want you to meet the sweetest little thing in the whole wide world.*

Music and applause as HELTON holds out his hand to MARY. Suddenly HARPO springs between them from the centre of the wreath and strikes a pose, holding his hooter, a rose clasped between his teeth. MARY backs off, while HELTON looks amazed.

Shot of the scene as the two thugs in evening dress rush forward and carry HARPO off.

We see them again from the drawing room door as they hustle him out, his feet waving in the air, gleefully sounding his hooter. Camera pans as they exit.

In a corner of the drawing room, GROUCHO stops the BUTLER as he passes carrying a champagne bottle and some glasses on a tray.

BUTLER : *Oh! Oh, no, sir. This is special for Mr. Helton, sir.*

GROUCHO pulling out a note : *You see this?*

The BUTLER grins and looks round furtively, while GROUCHO

74

pours himself a glass of champagne and drinks.

GROUCHO holding up the note again : *Come back in a half hour and I'll give you another look at it.* He exits.

The scene changes to the terrace outside the house. BRIGGS is prowling to and fro beneath it as GROUCHO comes out of the french windows and reclines on top of the balustrade.

A closer shot as BRIGGS comes up to him. He sits up.

BRIGGS : *Listen, keep your eye on Helton. We're gonna grab his daughter and take her to the old barn.*

GROUCHO : *Old barn? A fine tinhorn sport you are. With all the good shows in town, taking a girl to an old barn!* Nose in air : *Huh!*

BRIGGS : *Once we get hold of that girl, he'll take orders from me, and believe me, I'll show him who's . . .*

GROUCHO : *Enough of this small talk! Where's your wife, Lucille?*

BRIGGS angrily : *Would you . . .* He turns. *Shhhh. Someone's coming. I'll be back.*

GROUCHO seizing him by the wrist : *All right, be back next Thursday and bring a specimen of your handwriting, and above all, don't worry!*

BRIGGS : *Aww!* He exits with an angry gesture.

We now see LUCILLE in the garden, looking from side to side. GROUCHO, in medium close-up, climbs back onto the balustrade and starts acting like a tomcat.

GROUCHO : *Miaow!*

LUCILLE, in the garden, turns at the sound.

GROUCHO off : *Miaow!*

Resume on him on all fours, prowling to and fro on the balustrade.

GROUCHO : *Mia-a-a-ow.*

Camera pans with LUCILLE as she hurries across the garden and up onto the terrace.

GROUCHO off : *Mia-a-a-ow. Miaow!*

She passes behind him, going towards the house.

A closer shot of GROUCHO on the balustrade. He wiggles his behind and miaows again.

GROUCHO : *Mia-a-a-ow!*

He jumps down as LUCILLE comes up to him.

LUCILLE : *What brought you here?*

GROUCHO dramatically : *Ah, 'tis midsummer madness, the music is in my temples, the hot blood of youth! Come, Kapellmeister, let the violas throb. My regiment leaves at dawn!**

Bugle and drums off. LUCILLE throws off her wrap and GROUCHO takes her in his arms.

Music over a shot of the scene as they waltz round and round the terrace, fall over a couch, then get up again.

They dance back to back, then waltz towards the couch again — and fall straight over the end.

Cut to medium close-up as they land. A bugle sounds off.

GROUCHO : *Aw, I guess my regiment can go without me!*

Seen in a medium shot, they sit up on the couch. GROUCHO grabs LUCILLE and tries to kiss her.

LUCILLE pushing him away : *Oh, no, no, no, don't. My husband might be inside, and if he finds me out here he'll wallop me.*

A closer shot of the two of them. She smooths her hair.

---

* S. J. Perelman, the co-author of the script, says that this was the beginning of a long Stroheim parody speech, which Groucho cut out with his usual remark when he was worried that a joke might be too rarefied : ' The barber won't get that in Peru ' — meaning Peru, Indiana, of course.

GROUCHO : *Always thinking of your husband. Couldn't I wallop you just as well?*

LUCILLE : *Oh, I heard Alky talking about this party.*

GROUCHO putting an arm round her : *Oh, I've dreamed of a night like this, I tell you. Now you tell me about some of your dreams.*

LUCILLE : *Dreams! Ha! I can't even sleep any more wondering who he's chasing around with.*

GROUCHO expansively : *Oh, why can't we break away from all this, just you and I, and lodge with my fleas in the hills* . . . She looks at him doubtfully . . . *I mean flee to my lodge in the hills.*

Camera tilts as she rises.

LUCILLE : *Oh, no, I couldn't think of it.*

GROUCHO also rising : *Don't be afraid. You can join this lodge for a few pennies, and you won't even have to take a physical examination, unless you insist on one.*

Resume on the previous shot. She sits down and he sits under her.

Then we cut back to the closer shot again.

LUCILLE chin on hand : *What a swell home life I've got.* She turns

77

and leans over him. *Why, I think I'd almost marry you to spite that double-crossing crook.*

Resume on the medium shot as they rise and GROUCHO stands with his hands on her shoulders.

GROUCHO : *Mrs. Briggs, I've known and respected your husband Alky for many years . . . and what's good enough for him is good enough for me.*

He suddenly throws himself down on the couch, dragging LUCILLE with him.

LUCILLE : *Ughh!*

We now see a couple in evening dress emerge from the french windows onto the terrace; camera pans as they walk towards the balustrade, revealing GROUCHO and LUCILLE hiding on the couch.

The couple are seen from beyond the balustrade as they come up to it; in the background, GROUCHO and LUCILLE lean forward to listen.

MAN looking round nervously : *Oh, Emily!*

He grabs her in his arms. GROUCHO climbs onto the couch to get a better view.

WOMAN : *Oh, Henry, be careful. Somebody may see us.*

MAN hungrily : *Oh, I've been careful too long.*

GROUCHO : *Well, now that you've brought that up, just how long have you been careful?*

They whip round.

WOMAN : *Oh, they saw us!*

MAN : *Now, be calm, Emily. I'll talk to them.* To GROUCHO : *You won't say anything about this, will you?*

GROUCHO drawing himself up : *Sir, are you trying to offer me a bribe? . . . How much?*

WOMAN : *Oh, but you don't understand. You see, I'm not happy with my husband.* Scornfully : *He should have married some little housewife!*

GROUCHO, in close-up, wags a finger.

GROUCHO : *Madam, I resent that. Some of my best friends are housewives.* He works his eyebrows at LUCILLE.

LUCILLE, in close-up, smooths her hair.

LUCILLE : *Ahem!*

We see GROUCHO standing over the couple again.

MAN : *Now see here, if you're going to talk like that . . .*
GROUCHO : *Listen here, you're living in a fool's paradise. You intend to spend ten dollars and buy this woman a ring? Look at this.* He holds up a ring. *It's solid brass and a buck and a half takes it away. What do you say? . . . I know it'll fit her. I got it from the nose of a savage.*
MAN indignant : *Wh . . .!*
GROUCHO : *Well?*
WOMAN indignant : *Oh!*

Shot of the group.
GROUCHO : *You can have it for a dollar.*

The couple exit indignantly and GROUCHO shouts after them :
GROUCHO : *Fifty cents and not a nickel under!*

He pats LUCILLE on the head and steps down from the couch.
GROUCHO : *Now then, my friends, what am I offered for this fine piece of French bric-a-brac?*

A closer shot of the two of them as he sits down beside her.
LUCILLE : *Oh, I know what it is to be unhappy.*
GROUCHO : *How do you think I feel? Here I am stuck with this ring.*
LUCILLE disgustedly : *I've been married for four years. Four years of neglect, four years of battling, four years of heartbreak . . .*

The two of them are seen in medium close-up.
GROUCHO : *That makes twelve years. You must have been married in rompers . . . Mighty pretty country round there. You think you'll ever go back?* He tries to draw her down on the couch. *Come here, babe, I like you.*
LUCILLE pulling away : *Oh, I shouldn't. What about my husband?*
GROUCHO : *That's all right. Maybe we can get a girl for him.*

LUCILLE looks off and gives a little scream.
LUCILLE : *Ohh!*

Shot of the scene as she grabs her wrap and runs off in the foreground, while BRIGGS runs up in the background. GROUCHO tries to hide under a cushion, but BRIGGS comes and grabs it.
BRIGGS standing over him : *Who was that? My wife?*
GROUCHO : *Married to her twelve years and you have to ask me?*
BRIGGS : *What are you doing out here? I thought I told you to spy on Helton.*
GROUCHO : *I did spy on him.*
BRIGGS : *What was he doing?*

GROUCHO : *He was spying on me.*
BRIGGS : *Did he see you?*
GROUCHO : *No. I was too foxy for him. All he could do was spy on me.*
BRIGGS : *Well, get back in there. We're all set to cop his girl.*
GROUCHO : *Okay, chief.*

BRIGGS runs off in the background again, and we cut to a closer shot of GROUCHO as he pulls out a cigar and leans back. His hand lights the cigar with a lighter.

He throws away the lighter and settles himself on the couch, smoking.

Out in the garden, a girl appears, running across the lawns. Camera pans as HARPO chases her on a bicycle. The girl screams.

We return to the interior of the drawing room; the band is seen at one end of the room as CHICO enters through the french windows in the background.

In a closer shot, camera pans as he comes up and taps the pianist on the arm.

CHICO : *Hey! They gotta some good stuff outside. You wanna drink?*

The pianist nods and exits.

Shot of CHICO as he sits down at the piano.

CHICO : *Ready, boys?* He raps the piano. *Let's go.*

He starts to play the divertissement from Delibes' *Sylvia*.

Camera shows his hands on the keyboard as he plays with his forefinger.

Then we resume on him as he hurries to the end of the piece.

CHICO to the other musicians : *Ha-ha. I beat you that time.*

He starts playing again, ending up with ' Ain't she sweet? '.

There is applause as he finishes and he turns in surprise.

Reverse shot of the guests, who have gathered round, applauding.

CHICO, at the piano, bows, then leaves.

We move to the doorway leading into the drawing room. HELTON comes through accompanied by a very tall woman in a frilled dress with an enormous bustle.

HELTON : *Mary's swell. Say, let me get you a glass of punch.*

WOMAN : *I'd love it.*

Camera pans as they cross to the punch bowl; the bustle follows a few feet behind.

In a closer shot, HELTON and the woman raise their cups and drink. HARPO's head emerges from the bustle, looks to and fro, then disappears again.

WOMAN : *Just what I needed, Joe.* She takes HELTON's arm.

HELTON : *Ah!*

Resume on the previous shot as the band starts playing and HELTON and the woman exit, leaving the bustle behind. HARPO looks out again and grins.

We see couples dancing in the drawing room. HARPO comes up in the bustle and attaches himself to a dancing woman. She turns and cries out.

WOMAN : *Ohhh!*

Shot of HELTON standing at the side of the room as CHICO comes up and taps him on the shoulder.

HELTON affably : *Well, well, how're they coming, kid?*

CHICO : *Fine.*

HELTON : *Getting everything you want?*
A closer shot of both.
CHICO : *Sure, but how about a job for my grandfather?*
HELTON : *Your grandfather? What does he do?*
CHICO : *He puts cheese in-a moustraps.*
HELTON : *Why, we haven't got any mice here.*
CHICO : *Oh, 'at'sa all right. He brings his own mice with him.*
HELTON laughs and slaps him on the shoulder.
HARPO is meanwhile sitting on the couch by the balustrade at the end of the room, enveloped in the bustle. A girl in fancy dress passes; HARPO throws aside the bustle and chases her round and round, leaping over the balustrade. They finally run off. The band continues to play.
We follow MARY and ZEPPO as the music ends and they come to a halt by the doorway into the hall. There is a buzz of voices.
ZEPPO : You know, Mary, everyone seems to be having nearly as much fun as I am.
The BUTLER comes up to them from the hall.
BUTLER : *I beg your pardon, but there's someone to see you, Miss Helton.*
MARY to ZEPPO : *Pardon me a minute, and I'll hurry right back.*
ZEPPO : *Surely.*
MARY goes into the hall.
We see SHORTY, BUTCH and SPIKE rise from the band and start out with determined expressions.
In the hall, HARPO chases a girl in a short skirt down the stairs. The girl runs past another in a fairy godmother costume who is standing at the bottom.
In a closer shot, HARPO stops by the second girl and whistles. She turns towards him.
Resume on the scene as he jumps on the panière of her skirt and it collapses; he beats down the other side, messes her head-dress and exits gleefully.
In the drawing room, GROUCHO stands wearing a jockey cap, surrounded by a crowd of admiring girls. One of them strokes his chest.
GROUCHO : *No, you're wrong, girls. You're wrong. In the first place, Gary Cooper is much taller than I am.*

GIRL : *Ohhh!*

HELTON comes up and hands GROUCHO a piece of paper.

HELTON : *I wish you'd announce this singer. I can't make out the name.*

He exits and GROUCHO steps forward, tearing up the piece of paper.

GROUCHO : *Ladies and gentlemen.*

A closer shot of him.

GROUCHO : *I wish to announce that a buffet supper will be served in the next room in five minutes. In order to get you in that room quickly, Mrs. Schmalhausen will sing a soprano solo in this room.*
He gestures off.

We see a tall, well-developed lady standing beside the piano. She sings, accompanied by a female harpist.

WOMAN singing : ' *Que bella cosa 'na iurnata'e sole*
　　　　　　　N'aria serena doppo 'na tempesta.'

HARPO appears behind the harp and grins through it at the harpist, who exits with a scream.

A closer shot shows HARPO grinning through the harp strings, gibbering like an ape.

WOMAN singing, off : ' *Pe' ll'aria fresca . . .*'

Resume on the scene as HARPO takes the harpist's place and starts to accompany the singer.

WOMAN singing : '. . . *pare gia 'na festa* '

HARPO's hand gets stuck in the harp; he disengages it.

WOMAN singing : ' *Che bella cosa 'na iurnata'e . . .*'

Shot of HARPO; he unscrews the false hand, scratches his chin with it and throws it away. Then he rolls up his sleeve and continues playing.

WOMAN singing, off : 　　　　'. . . *sole.*
　　　　　Ma n'atu sole cchiu bello chine'
　　　　　O sole mio stan' frontea te '

HARPO plucks too hard and hits himself on the chin.

WOMAN singing, off : ' *O sole, o sole mio, sta'n frontea te*
　　　　　Sta'n . . .'

Back to the scene.

WOMAN singing : '. . . *frontea te.*'

HARPO rises to take a bow.

Resume on the previous shot. He sits down hurriedly as the

83

woman continues to sing, and drops the harp on his foot. He rubs his foot, scratches the sole of his shoe, then continues playing.

WOMAN singing, off : ' *Ma n'atu sole cchiu bello ohine* ' '

HARPO thumbs his nose at the woman as he plays.

WOMAN singing, off : ' *O sole mio, sta'n frontea te.* '

He clicks his nose as he plucks at the strings.

WOMAN singing, off : ' *O sole, o sole mio, sta'n frontea te Sta'n frontea . . .* '

The singer starts a high-pitched trill. HARPO looks alarmed and tugs wildly at one of the base strings of the harp.

We see the singer, trilling.

HARPO stuffs his fingers in his ears, looks round for his hat and puts it on.

In a shot of the scene, HARPO finally flings his coat over his head as he plays the final bars.

WOMAN trilling : '. . . *te.* '

She finally makes it to the end of the song. Loud applause; she bows and exits, and HARPO waves his arms in relief.

We see CHICO among the applauding guests. He steps forward and goes off.

He comes up to the grinning HARPO, by the musicians.

CHICO : *Hey, 'at'sa no good. You want to get thrown out again? Play something nice. I tell you what to play. Play . . .*

He sings the tune of ' Sugar in the morning . . .'. HARPO gets it, whistles along, then grabs a seat and starts to play the tune on the harp.

CHICO : *'At'sa it. Ah, 'at's beautiful. 'At'sa magnifico. Umm, boy, I like that.* He leaves.

A closer shot of HARPO playing. The orchestra accompanies him to the end of the piece. Applause off.

HARPO, in close-up, grins; the frog croaks inside his hat, moving the crown up and down.

By the doorway into the hall, the guests stand applauding while one of them beckons wildly to HELTON off-screen. (It is the man GROUCHO accosted on the terrace earlier.) HELTON hurries in and the man speaks in his ear.

HELTON wildly : *Oh! Oh! Mary! They've kidnapped her!*

ZEPPO runs in.

ZEPPO : *Who's been kidnapped?*
HELTON : *Mary! My daughter! Do something!*
ZEPPO : *Well, who could have done it?*
HELTON : *It's that Alky Briggs.*

A closer shot as HELTON goes up to the man who called him over.

HELTON : *You saw them drag her into the car. Where did they take her? Where did they take her?*
MAN : *Well, you see, first they blindfolded me, and then they turned me around this way . . .*

GROUCHO enters.

GROUCHO : *Of course, of course. They took her to the barn. Say, fellows, let's all pack up a nice little lunch and go down to the old barn, eh?*

The two thugs in evening dress enter from the hall.

HELTON : *Red, you go down to the North Road.* One of the thugs runs off. *Jack, you head down by Front Street. I'll go and pick up a couple of the boys. Come on! Come on!*
GROUCHO : *And I'll stay here and pick up a couple of dames.*

Shot of the scene as the guests all pour out into the hall and CHICO appears in the foreground.

GROUCHO taking off his jacket : *This is no time for women. On to the barn!*

HARPO comes up, hops on the back of the tall woman in the frilled dress and rides out.

CHICO turning in the doorway : *Gee, I wish I had a horse!*

They all exit, to the sound of HARPO's hooter.

The scene changes to the exterior of the old barn, in darkness. A car drives up and BRIGGS and his henchmen hustle MARY into the barn.

BRIGGS : *Hurry up. Come on.*

The car drives off.

Inside the barn, they enter through the door, MARY struggling between BUTCH and SPIKE.

MARY : *Let me go! Let me go! Let me go!*
BRIGGS : *No use yelling, kid. Nobody'll hear you here.*

Pan as they cross the floor amid piles of hay and cartwheels.

MARY : *You wait until my father hears about this.*

85

BRIGGS pausing: *Well, he's gonna hear about it, because I'm gonna tell him myself.* MARY struggles wildly. *Listen, take it easy. You're not goin' any place. Don't get all excited. Come on.*

MARY: *You take your hands off me, I tell you.*

BUTCH: *Go on!*

They arrive at the bottom of some stairs leading up to the loft.

BRIGGS: *Listen, kid, nobody's gonna hurt you. You'll be out of here in an hour if your old man comes through ... Butch, you take care of the girl while I telephone Joe. Come on, you guys.*

BUTCH hauls her screaming up the stairs, while camera pans with BRIGGS, SPIKE and SHORTY as they go to the door and exit.

We follow BUTCH from a low angle as he carries MARY along the gallery at the top of the stairs.

MARY: *Don't! Stop! Stop!*

In a room in the loft, BUTCH carries MARY in through the door and deposits her on a chair. She screams and struggles.

MARY: *You take your hands off me!*

BUTCH roughly: *Now, make yourself at home, but shut up!*

Pan as he goes to the door.

Outside the barn a taxi drives up and stops.

We see the driver in the foreground as GROUCHO and CHICO get out on the other side.

DRIVER: *Dollar-ten.*

GROUCHO holding out a note: *Here's a dollar. Keep the change.*

DRIVER: *But I said a dollar-ten.*

GROUCHO grabbing back the note: *All right. Give me the dollar. I'll keep the change.*

They walk away.

CHICO to GROUCHO: *That's half a dollar I owe you.*

In a longer shot, the taxi drives off and they go up to the barn door in the background.

At the door, CHICO and GROUCHO enter from foreground and turn to face camera; GROUCHO is carrying a picnic basket.

CHICO: *You call this a barn? This looks like a stable.*

A closer shot of the two of them.

GROUCHO: *Well, if you look at it, it's a barn. If you smell it, it's a stable.*

CHICO: *Well, let's just look at it.*

Seen from below, BUTCH leans out of the loft window above them. He bellows threateningly :

BUTCH : *Get out of here!*

GROUCHO and CHICO start and look upwards.

GROUCHO : *Say, have you got a girl up in that hay loft?*

BUTCH off : *No.*

GROUCHO : *Then you're a bigger fool than I thought you were.*

We see BUTCH holding up a sack.

BUTCH : *Beat it, I tell you!*

Back to the other two.

GROUCHO : *What'd you say?*

Resume on BUTCH at the window.

BUTCH : *I said beat it.* He throws down the sack.

The sack whistles down and lands with a crash by GROUCHO and CHICO.

A closer shot of the two of them.

GROUCHO dead pan : *Pardon me. What did you say?*

BUTCH off : *I said beat it.*

GROUCHO : *He said beat it. Gee, I wish I'd said that. Everybody's repeating it around the club.*

A closer shot of BUTCH at the window.

BUTCH : *I'm coming down to get you.* He goes inside.

Resume on CHICO and GROUCHO.

GROUCHO : *Don't bother. We'll come right up.* He picks up the picnic basket and says to CHICO : *Come on, I'm going in to get him.*

We move to the interior of the old barn. CHICO and GROUCHO enter in the background and walk towards us. Hens cluck; a cow moos loudly off-screen.

In a closer shot, camera pans as they walk across and sit down on a pile of hay.

GROUCHO : *Well, here we are in the old barn, all set for a nice picnic lunch.* He opens the picnic basket. *Oh gosh, the picnic is off. We haven't got any red ants.*

CHICO chewing a bit of hay : *I know an Indian who's got a couple of red aunts ...*

GROUCHO pulls out a napkin and lays it on the ground.

CHICO : *Hey, don't you think we'd better go look for the girl?*

GROUCHO : *Let's wait till we get through eating. There's hardly enough lunch for two.*

87

CHICO : *I don't see why she couldn't get kidnapped near a restaurant.*

GROUCHO pulling out some plates : *Some dark night I think I'll come here and lay for you if the hens don't get sore.* He hands CHICO a tin cup. *Here, go over to that filling station and get some milk — Grade A.*

> Shot of the scene. There is a cow in the background, and as CHICO turns, a calf runs up to it and starts to suckle. The cow moos.
>
> Resume on the two men as GROUCHO pulls food out of the basket.

GROUCHO : *Well, come on, come on, where's the milk?*

CHICO : *There's a customer ahead of me.*

> Camera follows BUTCH from a low angle as he walks along the gallery of the loft, then we cut to a shot of the scene as he looks down.

BUTCH : *Hey!*

> GROUCHO and CHICO rise.
>
> A closer shot of BUTCH, from below.

BUTCH : *What're you doin' here?*

> We see CHICO and GROUCHO, looking up.

GROUCHO : *What are we doing? What about you, kidnapping a girl! Nice old-fashioned bit of melodrama, kidnapping a girl!* He wags a finger. *You've been reading too many dime novels.*

CHICO : *Go on, you get 'im. I'll wait for you outside.*

> In a shot of the scene, CHICO stands aside as GROUCHO starts for the stairs.
>
> Then we resume on BUTCH.

BUTCH savagely : *Keep out of this loft!*

> Back to the other two, GROUCHO on the stairs.

CHICO : *Well, it's better to have loft and lost, then never to have loft at all.*

GROUCHO patting him on the shoulder : *Nice work!*

> Resume on BUTCH.

BUTCH : *Beat it, or I'll t'row you out.* He runs off.

> Camera pans with BUTCH as, having come down the stairs, he chases the others across the barn and round one of the posts supporting the gallery. Hens scatter, clucking, and the cow moos as he trips over a bale of straw, while GROUCHO starts

up a ladder.

In a longer shot, GROUCHO and CHICO climb the ladder to the loft. BUTCH pokes CHICO from below with a pitchfork and follows them up. They leap over the edge onto a pile of hay and BUTCH starts back down the ladder.

At the bottom, we follow BUTCH as he comes down and throws himself into the pile of hay.

Meanwhile, up in the loft, MARY runs across and pulls frantically at the locked door.

CHICO emerges from the pile of hay and starts up the ladder again, pursued by BUTCH.

At that moment the door opens and HARPO runs in. We follow him as he runs across the stable, seizing a pitchfork. BUTCH laughs off-screen, and CHICO shouts:

CHICO off : *Take your face out of my foot!*

BUTCH off : *I gotcha! Now I gotcha!*

HARPO now arrives at the bottom of the ladder and jabs BUTCH in the backside with the pitchfork. BUTCH comes down the ladder and advances threateningly on HARPO, who jabs him in the chest. BUTCH puts up his hands while CHICO descends from the ladder.

CHICO tweaking his face : *So, thought we were afraid, hey? Thought we were afraid, did ya!*

A closer shot as BUTCH seizes the pitchfork and breaks it slowly into pieces.

At that moment, ZEPPO comes in through the door and looks round.

BUTCH off : *Now I'm goin' to give it to you guys right!*

Camera pans as ZEPPO runs across the stable.

Arriving at the bottom of the ladder, he knocks out BUTCH. Animal noises off.

A closer shot as MARY screams from the loft; ZEPPO looks up and runs off, while CHICO and HARPO seize BUTCH's feet.

Camera follows ZEPPO from below as he runs up the stairs and along the gallery.

We see MARY locked in the loft as ZEPPO bursts in through the door.

Down below, HARPO and CHICO hide behind the barn door as BRIGGS bursts in with SHORTY and SPIKE, to find BUTCH laid out cold.

BRIGGS bending over him : *Butch! Butch, what happened?* Looking up : *Hey!*

Up in the gallery, ZEPPO and MARY turn and look round, then we cut back to the barn floor.

BRIGGS : *You get out of that loft!*

Seen from below, ZEPPO vaults over the edge of the gallery to the top of the stairs.

In a long shot, he leaps from the head of the stairs and lands on BRIGGS. They roll over in the hay. MARY screams off.

Resume on the scene by the door as SHORTY and SPIKE lean over BUTCH's recumbent figure.

SHORTY : *What's happened, old man?*

SPIKE : *Come out of here. Come out of here, Butch.*

As they pull him up from the floor, HARPO and CHICO emerge from behind the door and knock them out.

We see ZEPPO and BRIGGS fighting. ZEPPO hits BRIGGS . . .

BRIGGS lands on the hay pile; ZEPPO follows. They roll over and vanish, as GROUCHO rises from the hay.

GROUCHO : *Where's all those farmer's daughters I've been hearing about for years?* He disappears into the hay again.

Resume on ZEPPO and BRIGGS fighting. BRIGGS hits ZEPPO . . . ZEPPO lands on the hay pile; BRIGGS follows, and they roll over hitting one another. GROUCHO rises from the hay behind them.

GROUCHO : *Hey, why don't you boys fight over there? You wanna break my glasses?* He gets up and goes off.

We see BRIGGS's three henchmen laid out on the floor. CHICO is standing by a wagon wheel fixed to the wall behind.

CHICO : *Come on, folks, step right up. Only ten cents a chance.*

HARPO enters and gives him a coin.

CHICO : *Attaboy. Here you are.* He spins the wheel. *Ten cents gets you . . . look at that. The only game in the stable.* The wheel stops. *Let's see. Number sixteen wins. The lucky number. There you are, young man.*

He hands HARPO an iron bar. HARPO coshes SPIKE as he sits up groggily, and he falls back on the floor again.

CHICO taking back the bar : *Sorry you didn't get a better one.*

We see ZEPPO and BRIGGS still fighting, then cut back to the wagon wheel. CHICO spins it a second time.

CHICO : *Here we go. Let's see what comes up.* The wheel stops. *Well, well, if he isn't the lucky guy . . . Double O, two shots for the price of one.*

He hands the iron bar to HARPO, who coshes SHORTY as he rises.

CHICO : *Folks, this is the best game in all . . .*

HARPO, carried away, hits him too and he falls.

We return to ZEPPO and BRIGGS fighting.

Then camera pans with GROUCHO as he goes across to the cow and its suckling calf.

GROUCHO : *You're a mother, you understand. How would you like to have somebody steal one of your heifers? I know, heifer cow is better than none, but this is no time for puns.* Pointing : *Get in that battle over there.* He runs off.

ZEPPO knocks down BRIGGS at the bottom of the stairs . . .

While GROUCHO starts a running commentary, standing in an old buggy and talking into a carriage lamp.

GROUCHO : *Well, here we are again at the ringside, folks, it looks like a great battle. Now the boys are locked in the centre of the ring. Oh, baby, what a grudge fight!*

Sounds of punching. GROUCHO leaps up and down in the buggy.

GROUCHO : *Zowie! Zowie! Zowie! That makes three zowies, and a man gets a base on balls.*

Dust showers down on him from the canopy of the buggy.

GROUCHO : *Ending of the first inning, no runs, no errors, but plenty of hits. Whee!* He steps out of the buggy.

Resume on the other two as the fighting continues. ZEPPO hits BRIGGS, who grunts with pain.

GROUCHO is now seen perched on a cross beam up by the gallery. He talks into a watering can.

GROUCHO : *This programme is coming to you through the courtesy of the Golden Goose Furniture Company with three stores — 125th Street, 125th Street and 125th Street. You furnish the girl, we tar and feather your nest. Look for our advertisement in today's ash can.*

He resumes his commentary, to sounds of fighting off-screen.

GROUCHO : *Now the boys are at it in the centre of the ring. Oh!*

That one hurt! Waving the watering can : *Come on, you palookas,
stop stalling. Oh, mama, if I only had my youth again. Wheee!*
He steps along the beam.

Down below, BRIGGS hits ZEPPO, and the fight continues.

We see HARPO sitting backwards on a horse. Hand thrust in
shirt-front à la Napoleon, he watches the fight through an old
bottle used as a telescope, and points fiercely, directing the
battle. The horse whinnies.

Resume on the fight. BRIGGS hits ZEPPO again.

CHICO is seen sitting on a cow. He sounds its bell and calls out :
CHICO : *Round two.*

BRIGGS and ZEPPO grapple by the staircase . . .

While GROUCHO continues his commentary, perched up in the
roof.

GROUCHO into the watering can : *Both boys are fiddling in the
middle of the ring. and I don't think much of the tune.* The cows
moo. *Briggs is bobbing and weaving. It's nice work if you can get
it. Now they're trying — very trying.* Sounds of punching off. *I
copped that one from an almanac. Now they're in the centre of the
ring and the crowd hurrahs!*

Shot of a cow. It moos loudly.

BRIGGS raises a chair above his head . . .

Camera pans with ZEPPO as he falls across the floor.

BRIGGS advances with the chair raised, and we cut to a shot
of the scene as he brings it down on ZEPPO.

At that moment HELTON comes in through the door.

BRIGGS picks up ZEPPO and hits him. ZEPPO hits BRIGGS . . .

Camera pans as he falls backwards . . .

And lands on his back amid a pile of old chairs.

Meanwhile MARY rushes down the staircase and into HELTON's
arms, watched by ZEPPO.

MARY : *Oh, dad!*

HELTON : *Are you all right, honey?*

Beside them HARPO emerges from the hay pile, clutching the
calf. It's bell rings.

Seen in closer shot, HARPO gleefully kisses the calf.

HELTON off : *Good boy . . .*

Camera pans to show him shaking ZEPPO by the hand,

HELTON : *Remember, old Joe Helton . . .*

Shot of the scene.

HELTON : ... *never forgot a friend.*

ZEPPO : *Well, this was one job that certainly was a pleasure.*

HELTON : *Ah!* He laughs.

ZEPPO and MARY exit arm in arm, to a chorus of cow bells and animal noises. HELTON turns to find GROUCHO by the hay pile, pitching hay in the air.

HELTON : *What are you doing?*

GROUCHO : *I'm looking for a needle in a haystack.*

Fade out to the music of ' Sugar in the morning . . .'
Fade in . . . THE END . . . Fade out.

CREDITS :

Screenplay by	Bert Kalmar and Harry Ruby
Additional dialogue by	Arthur Sheekman and Nat Perrin
Director of photography	Henry Sharp
Art direction	Hans Dreier and Wiard B. Ihnen
Edited by	LeRoy Stone
Music and lyrics by	Bert Kalmar and Harry Ruby
Musical director	Arthur Johnston
Running time	68 or 70 minutes
Released by	Paramount, 17 November, 1933

CAST :

Rufus T. Firefly	Groucho
Pinky	Harpo
Chicolini	Chico
Bob Roland	Zeppo
Mrs Teasdale	Margaret Dumont
Vera Marcal	Raquel Torres
Trentino	Louis Calhern
Lemonade vendor	Edgar Kennedy
Zander	Edmund Breese
Secretary	Verna Hillie
Agitator	Leonid Kinsky
Judge	George MacQuarrie
Secretary of War	Edwin Maxwell
Prosecutor	Charles B. Middleton
Minister of Finance	William Worthington

DUCK SOUP

Music as the credits come up over a shot of some ducks swimming in a cauldron over a fire, then fade in to a flag waving from a mast. The word FREEDONIA appears over it, then we wipe to a shot of Freedonia itself — a small Ruritanian town with steeply pitched roofs and church steeples.

The music ends as a diagonal wipe transports us to the council chamber of the Freedonian government where the president, ZANDER, and his cabinet are in session. Camera follows ZANDER as he walks across to MRS TEASDALE on the left.

ZANDER : *Mrs Teasdale.*

MRS TEASDALE : *Yes, your Excellency?*

ZANDER : *I again ask you to reconsider.*

Shot of MRS TEASDALE and a minister.

MRS TEASDALE decisively : *Gentlemen, I've already loaned Freedonia more than half the fortune my husband left me.* We lose the minister as she walks to the right. *I consider that money lost, and now you're asking for another twenty million dollars.*

The cabinet stand in consternation as she walks away to the window.

A MINISTER following : *But it would only be for a few months to meet this present emergency.*

They are now seen across the council table; camera pans as they pursue MRS TEASDALE.

MINISTER : *With twenty million dollars in the treasury, we can announce an immediate reduction in taxes.* They stop. *That's all the people are asking for.*

MRS TEASDALE : *I'm sorry, but I'm inclined to agree with the people. The government has been mismanaged.*

ZANDER starting forward : *What?*

A longer shot of the group.

MRS TEASDALE : *I will lend the money, but only on condition that His Excellency withdraw and place the government in new hands.*

As she speaks, the other members of the council get up from their places and gather round, and we cut in to a medium shot.

95

ZANDER : *You ask me to give up my office?*
MRS TEASDALE : *Yes, your Excellency. In a crisis like this I feel Freedonia needs a new leader.* Dramatically : *A progressive, fearless fighter, a man like Rufus T. Firefly.*
Back to the longer shot.
A MINISTER : *Rufus T. Firefly?*
MRS TEASDALE : *I will lend the money . . .*
Back to the previous shot again.
MRS TEASDALE : *. . . to Freedonia only if Firefly is appointed leader.*
Music as we dissolve to a newspaper headline which reads : FIREFLY APPOINTED NEW LEADER OF FREE-DONIA.
Dissolve again to a picture of FIREFLY, with cigar.
Then to another newspaper which reads :

MAMMOTH RECEPTION ARRANGED TO
WELCOME NATION'S LEADER TONIGHT
SELECTION OF RUFUS T. FIREFLY GREETED WITH CHEERS OF
FREEDONIANS

*Rufus T. Firefly will take over the reigns of the Freedonian
Government immediately. Firefly's sponsor, it was learned, is
Mrs Gloria Teasdale, wealthy widow of the late Chester V.
Teasdale, and from all reports the new leader will execute
his duties with an iron hand . . .*

The music fades as we dissolve to the ballroom where the
reception for FIREFLY is being held. Guests in evening dress
throng the floor. There is a fanfare of trumpets.

After another dissolve, we see the main staircase with the
entrance to the ballroom at the top, flanked by guards, and
the trumpeters in the background. Camera tracks in as a
LACKEY enters.

LACKEY announcing: *The Honorable Secretary of Finance and
party.*

The LACKEY exits and the SECRETARY OF FINANCE and his
party enter and start down the stairs. Track in again as the
LACKEY reappears; there is another fanfare.

LACKEY : *His Excellency, Ambassador Trentino of Sylvania.*

TRENTINO and his party enter, bowing; camera pans as they
come down and meet MRS TEASDALE on the staircase.

MRS TEASDALE : *Ambassador!*

TRENTINO : *Mrs. Teasdale!*

Music over a low angle shot of the two of them. One of
TRENTINO'S aides bows and exits.

MRS TEASDALE : *It was so good of you to come. I am anxious for
you to meet the new leader of our country.*

TRENTINO clasping her hand: *No matter who rules in Freedonia,
Mrs. Teasdale, to me you will always be the first lady of the land.*

He looks round as VERA MARCAL passes up the staircase; she
halts.

MRS TEASDALE : *Oh, permit me. This is Miss Vera Marcal.
Ambassador Trentino.*

TRENTINO kisses her hand with an air of complicity.

TRENTINO : *Miss Marcal needs no introduction. I've seen her dance
many times at the theatre.*

VERA : *Thank you.*

Seen from below, the trumpeters sound another fanfare and
the LACKEY re-enters.

LACKEY : *The Honorable Pandooh of Mufhtan.*

Resume on the trio, with the entrance in the background. Oriental music as the PANDOOH appears, wearing a turban.

MRS TEASDALE : *I must greet His Honour.*

She goes up the stairs to meet him, while TRENTINO takes VERA by the arm and walks her down the stairs towards camera.

We look down on the guests in the ballroom.

Then resume on TRENTINO and VERA as they sit down on the edge of the staircase.

TRENTINO in a half whisper : *What have you found out?*

VERA also half whispering : *Nothing. I've been waiting to hear from you.*

TRENTINO : *I've given up the idea of a revolution. I have a better plan.*

Music over a closer shot of the two of them.

VERA : *Oh, yes?*

TRENTINO : *I can gain control of Freedonia much easier by marrying Mrs. Teasdale.*

VERA laughing : *Maybe that's not going to be so easy.*
TRENTINO : *Eh?*
VERA : *Oh, from what I hear . . . You see, Mrs. Teasdale is rather sweet on this Rufus T. Firefly.*
The PANDOOH passes on the stairs behind them.
TRENTINO : *Oh! Well, that's where you come in.*
VERA : *Oh!*
TRENTINO : *I'm going to place him in your hands.*
VERA with relish : *Yes?*
TRENTINO leaning towards her : *I don't have to tell you what to do . . .*
VERA : *No.*
TRENTINO : *Or how to . . . Careful.*
Music over a shot of the scene. TRENTINO gets up as MRS TEASDALE and BOB enter down the stairs.
MRS TEASDALE : *I want you to meet his Excellency's secretary, Bob Roland — Ambassador Trentino.*
TRENTINO : *How do you do, sir.*
They shake hands.
BOB : *How do you do.*
MRS TEASDALE : *Miss Marcal.*
We now see the group from below. BOB bows to VERA and smiles.
BOB : *We've met.*
MRS TEASDALE : *Of course.*
TRENTINO acidly : *Well, I hope his Excellency gets here soon.*
BOB turning to him : *His Excellency makes it a point always to be on time. As long as I've known him, he's never been late for an appointment.* He sings : *His Excellency is due*
> *To take his station,*
> *Beginning his new administration*
> *He'll make his appearance when . . .*
He turns and points.
> *The clock on the wall . . .*
Camera pans to show the clock on the wall; it says just on ten.
BOB singing off : *. . . strikes ten.*
MRS TEASDALE singing off : *When the clock on the . . .*
Camera pans back to the group.

99

Mrs Teasdale singing : . . . *wall strikes ten,*
All you loyal ladies and you patriotic
men . . .

We look down on the whole ballroom, with Mrs Teasdale on the stairs in the background. Music.

Mrs Teasdale singing : *Let's sing the national anthem when*
The clock on the wall strikes ten.

Seen from below, the clock strikes ten. There is a roll of drums off-screen.

A long shot shows another entrance at the side of the ballroom, flanked with banners. Two trumpeters step forward and sound a fanfare, while guards with plumed helmets march into the ballroom. The guests all sing, accompanied by music.

Guests singing, off : *His Excellency is due*
To take his station,
Beginning his new administration.
He'll make his appearance when
The clock on the wall strikes ten.

The guards halt and face one another in two lines, then a troop of ballet dancers enter, scattering flowers. Camera tracks back.

Guests singing, off : *We'll give him a rousing cheer*
To show him we're glad that he's here.

A very high angle shot shows the guards and ballet girls flanking the staircase which leads up to the entrance.

Guests singing, off : *Hail, hail Freedonia!*

The trumpeters step forward and sound a fanfare while the ballet girls kneel and the guards draw their swords.

We see them again in a general shot as they stretch out their arms and swords towards the entrance.

Guests singing, off : *Hail, hail Freedonia!*
Land of the brave and free!

The music stops. Trentino, Mrs Teasdale, Vera and Bob stand with heads respectfully bowed, waiting for Firefly's entrance. Nothing happens. They straighten up and Trentino looks round.

The guards and ballet girls are still posed in welcome on the staircase.

Standing by the window, a row of trumpeters raise their

100

trumpets and sound a fanfare. The music starts again.
TRENTINO, MRS TEASDALE, VERA and BOB bow their heads again.
GUESTS singing, off : *Hail, hail* . . .
Resume on the guards and ballet girls, still posed in welcome.
GUESTS singing, off : . . . *Freedonia,*
> *Land of the brave and free.*

The music stops again as we cut to FIREFLY's bedroom, where he is lying asleep in bed, beneath the Freedonian flag. An alarm clock rings loudly.
FIREFLY wakes and leaps up in bed. He pulls off his night-shirt, revealing his clothes underneath, while the guests start singing again off-screen.
GUESTS singing, off : *Hail, hail, Freedonia.*
A longer shot of FIREFLY as he slides down a pole at the end of the bed and disappears from view.
GUESTS singing, off : *Land of the* . . .
Down in the ballroom, the guards and ballet girls are still gazing expectantly towards the entrance as FIREFLY comes sliding down the pole in the foreground and starts towards them.
GUESTS singing, off : . . . *brave and free.*
The music stops.
FIREFLY approaches one of the files of guards. He peers up the staircase, following their gaze, then crosses to the guards on the other side.
He tugs at the nearest guard's cuff, seen in medium close-up.
FIREFLY in an undertone : *You expecting somebody?*
GUARD out of the side of his mouth : *Yes.*
FIREFLY stands in line, his arm outstretched like the rest of them.
A medium shot now shows FIREFLY, the guards and balle girls, all gazing expectantly towards the entrance. The musi starts again.
GUESTS singing : *Hail, hail, Freedonia,*
> *Land* . . .

We see them from another angle as MRS TEASDALE enters in the background.
GUESTS singing : . . . *of the brave and free.*

101

The music ends. MRS TEASDALE spots FIREFLY and comes down the steps towards him.

MRS TEASDALE : *Oh, your Excellency!*

The guards retract their swords, the ballet girls their arms, and we cut to another shot of the group.

MRS TEASDALE : *We've been expecting you.* She gives him her hand and continues pompously : *As chairwoman of the reception committee, I extend the good wishes of every man, woman and child of Freedonia.*

She and FIREFLY are seen from a low angle.

FIREFLY : *Never mind that stuff. Take a card.*

He fans out a pack of cards.

MRS TEASDALE : *A card? What'll I do with a card?* She takes it.

FIREFLY : *You can keep it. I've got fifty-one left. Now, what were you saying?*

MRS TEASDALE pompously : *As chairwoman of the reception committee, I welcome you with open arms.*

FIREFLY : *Is that so? How late do you stay open?*

She looks at him dubiously but continues in the same tone :

MRS TEASDALE : *I've sponsored your appointment because I feel you are the most able statesman in all Freedonia.*

FIREFLY : *Well, that covers a lot of ground.* He looks her up and down. *Say, you cover a lot of ground yourself. You'd better beat it. I hear they're going to tear you down and put up an office building where you're standing. You can leave in a taxi. If you can't leave in a taxi you can leave in a huff. If that's too soon, you can leave in a minute and a huff. You know you haven't stopped talking since I came here? You must have been vaccinated with a phonograph needle.*

MRS TEASDALE grandiose : *The future of Freedonia rests on you. Promise me you'll follow in the footsteps of my husband.*

Close-up of FIREFLY.

FIREFLY to camera : *How do you like that? I haven't been on the job five minutes and already she's making advances to me.*

Resume on the two of them.

FIREFLY : *Not that I care, but where is your husband?*

MRS TEASDALE mournful : *Why, he's dead.*

FIREFLY : *I'll bet he's just using that as an excuse.*

MRS TEASDALE proudly : *I was with him to the very end.*

102

103

FIREFLY : *Huh! No wonder he passed away.*

MRS TEASDALE dramatically : *I held him in my arms and kissed him.*

FIREFLY : *Oh, I see. Then it was murder. Will you marry me? Did he leave you any money? Answer the second question first.*

MRS TEASDALE : *He left me his entire fortune.*

FIREFLY : *Is that so? Can't you see what I'm trying to tell you? I love you.*

Camera pans as he clasps her hands and circles round her.

MRS TEASDALE with a bashful smile : *Oh, your Excellency!*

FIREFLY : *You're not so bad yourself.* He works his eyebrows.

We cut to a medium shot as TRENTINO strides up to them.

MRS TEASDALE : *Oh, I want to present to you Ambassador Trentino of Sylvania . . .* FIREFLY offers him a card; he refuses . . . *Having him with us today is indeed a great pleasure.*

Camera tracks in on them.

TRENTINO : *Thank you, but I can't stay very long.*

FIREFLY turning his back : *That's an even greater pleasure.*

Shot of FIREFLY and TRENTINO.

FIREFLY : *Now, how about lending this country twenty million dollars, you old skinflint?* He puffs at his cigar.

TRENTINO : *Twenty million dollars is a lot of money. I should have to take that up with my Minister of Finance.*

FIREFLY : *Well, in the meantime, could you let me have twelve dollars until pay day?*

TRENTINO : *Twelve dollars?*

FIREFLY : *Don't be scared. You'll get it back. I'll give you my personal note for ninety days. If it isn't paid by then, you can keep the note.*

TRENTINO : *Your Excellency, haven't we seen each other somewhere before?*

FIREFLY : *I don't think so. I'm not sure I'm seeing you now. It must be something I ate.*

A warning hand is laid on his shoulder; camera pans to include MRS TEASDALE.

TRENTINO starting forward, indignant : *Look here, sir, are you trying to . . .*

FIREFLY looks round furtively.

FIREFLY : *Don't look now, but there's one man too many in this*

room . . . He taps TRENTINO on the chest . . . *and I think it's you.*
Cut to a longer shot as VERA enters in the background.

MRS TEASDALE to TRENTINO : *Oh, I'm so sorry.*

TRENTINO exits with a baffled bow to MRS TEASDALE. FIREFLY bows back.

MRS TEASDALE to FIREFLY : *I want you to meet a very charming lady.*

FIREFLY : *And it's about time.*

He makes off up the steps.

MRS TEASDALE : *Just a moment.*

He stops next to VERA, who laughs nervously.

MRS TEASDALE : *I want to present Miss Vera Marcal.*

Shot of the three of them.

FIREFLY : *Go ahead, I can take it.*

MRS TEASDALE with a laugh : *Oh, you don't understand. This is Vera Marcal, the famous dancer.*

FIREFLY : *Is that so?*

VERA : *Umm.*

FIREFLY : *Can you do this one?*

He dances, kicking up his legs. There is general laughter as we cut to a closer shot. The guests watch in the background.

FIREFLY : *I danced before Napoleon. No, Napoleon danced before me. In fact he danced two hundred years before me. Here's one I picked up in a dance hall.*

Resume on the previous shot as FIREFLY dances, flamenco style. The two women laugh.

FIREFLY is seen in medium close-up; then camera pans to include MRS TEASDALE.

FIREFLY pointing at her : *Here's another one I picked up in a dance hall.*

MRS TEASDALE indignant : *Oh!* She exits.

VERA enters, lays her hands on FIREFLY's shoulders and murmurs suggestively :

VERA : *Perhaps we get a chance to dance together, huh?*

FIREFLY : *I could dance with you till the cows come home.*

VERA : *Yes?*

FIREFLY : *On second thoughts, I'd rather dance with the cows till you came home.*

VERA starting back : *Huh!*

The group are seen from a low angle as VERA flings off in a huff.

FIREFLY : *Where's my secretary?*

BOB loudly, appearing on the right : *Here I am.*

FIREFLY nearly falls over and runs to hide behind MRS TEASDALE.

MRS TEASDALE : *Good heavens, your Excellency!*

FIREFLY recovers himself and strides to and fro.

FIREFLY : *Er . . . take a letter.*

BOB : *Who to?*

FIREFLY : *To my dentist.*

Medium close-up of FIREFLY.

FIREFLY : *Er . . . 'Dear Dentist: Enclosed find cheque for five hundred dollars. Yours very truly.' Send that off immediately.*

BOB off : *I'll . . . er . . . I'll have to enclose the cheque first.*

FIREFLY : *You do and I'll fire you.*

Resume on the group, with the guests watching in the background. BOB goes off.

MRS TEASDALE : *Your Excellency, the eyes of the world are upon*

106

you . . . FIREFLY starts hopping to and fro on one leg *. . . Notables from every country are gathered here in your honour. This is a gala day for you.*

FIREFLY : *Well, a gal a day is enough for me. I don't think I could handle any more.*

A closer shot of him and MRS TEASDALE.

MRS TEASDALE : *If it's not asking too much . . .* Music; she sings :
> *For our information,*
> *Just for illustration,*
> *Tell us how you intend*
> *To run the nation.*

Camera pans as FIREFLY steps forward, smoothing his hair, then follows him as he lopes to and fro, singing to the guests who surround him.

FIREFLY singing : *These are the laws of my administration.*
> *No one's allowed to smoke . . .*

In the ear of a blonde woman :
> *Or toll a dirty joke.*
> *And whistling is forbidden.*

He whistles and conducts the guests as they sing.

GUESTS singing : *We're not allowed to tell a dirty joke.*
> *Hail, hail Freedonia.*

FIREFLY singing : *If chewing gum is chewed*
> *The chewer is pursued,*
> *And in the hoose-gow hidden.*

He makes chewing motions.

GUESTS singing : *If we choose to chew, we'll be pursued.*

Pan as FIREFLY moves to another group of guests and addresses a grey-haired lady.

FIREFLY singing : *If any form of pleasure is exhibited.*
> *Report to me and it will be prohibited.*

Camera follows him from a high angle as he moves past some more guests and up to a girl.

FIREFLY singing : *I'll put my foot down,*
> *So shall it be.*
> *This is the land of the free.*

He takes the girl in his arms and goes on singing.
> *The last man nearly ruined this place,*
> *He didn't know what to do with it.*

> *If you think this country's bad off now,*
> *Just wait till I get through with it.*

He releases the girl.

We now see him with a group of generals and ministers behind him. Music as he dances a hornpipe, then cut to show him and a general.

FIREFLY wagging a finger at the general :

> *The country's taxes must be fixed,*
> *And I know what to do with it.*

We follow him to a group on the left.

> *If you think you're paying too much now,*
> *Just wait till I get through with it.*

Another shot of FIREFLY and the guests. He produces a piccolo and circles round, playing it. Everyone cheers and waves.

We see FIREFLY and a minister. FIREFLY leans on one of the guards' trumpets as he sings.

FIREFLY singing : *I will not stand for anything*
> *That's crooked or unfair.*

I'm strictly on the up and up,
So everyone beware.
If anyone's caught taking graft
And I don't get my share,
We stand 'em up against the wall . . .

He aims with the trumpet.

And pop goes the weasel!

We see him again with the guests. Camera pans as he dances round with the trumpet, singing 'Ah-ah-ah' in accompaniment to the guests.

GUESTS singing : *So everyone beware,*
Who's crooked or unfair,
No one must take a bit of graft
Unless he gets his share.

In a long shot of the scene, he goes up to a couple standing on the steps, the woman talking to a second man.

Cut to show the four of them as FIREFLY sings, gesturing from one to the other.

FIREFLY singing : *If any man should come between*
A husband and his bride,
We find out which one she prefers
By letting her decide.
If she prefers the other man,
The husband steps outside.
We stand him up against the wall,
And pop goes the weasel!

Camera pans with him as he lopes along, rolling up his trousers.

We see him again as he stands between two lackeys and sings 'Ah-ah-ah' again, along with the guests.

GUESTS singing : *The husband steps outside,*
Relinquishes his bride.

FIREFLY and the guests continue to sing, in a long shot of the scene.

FIREFLY : *Ah-ah-ah . . .*

GUESTS simultaneously : *They stand him up against the wall,*
And take him for a ride.

As they finish, resume on FIREFLY and the lackeys. FIREFLY stands with his mouth still open as MRS TEASDALE enters.

Mrs Teasdale : *You have an appointment at the House of Representatives.* She looks down. *Good heavens! You can't go with your trousers up.*

Firefly : *I can't eh? Well, they'll never catch me any other way. My car! His Excellency's car!*

A lackey is seen from below.

Lackey : *His Excellency's car!*

Then a trumpeter from a similar angle. He sounds a fanfare. Another lackey takes up the cry.

Lackey : *His Excellency's car!*

Another trumpeter sounds a fanfare.

Outside the palace, the guards stand in line at the gate.

Guards : *His Excellency's car!*

Another fanfare. In a closer shot, the guards stand aside while Pinky drives in through the gate on a motorcycle and sidecar and exits in the foreground.

High angle shot of the palace steps. The trumpets sound again as Pinky drives up on the motorcycle and squeals to a halt, with the Freedonian flag flying from the sidecar.

We now look up the palace steps to the entrance. In the foreground, PINKY crouches down by the motorcycle and takes a photograph as FIREFLY comes down flanked by two guards, who help him into the sidecar. The trumpeters sound another fanfare at the top of the steps.

PINKY puts away his camera and gets back on his motorcycle as FIREFLY orders him:

FIREFLY: *I'm in a hurry. To the House of Representatives. Ride like fury. If you run out of gas, get ethyl. If Ethyl runs out, get Mabel. Now, step on it!*

In a high angle shot the guards salute as PINKY roars off on the motorcycle — leaving FIREFLY and the sidecar behind. FIREFLY looks after him for a moment, then gets out.

We see him from below, with the guards still saluting.

FIREFLY nonchalantly: *Well, it certainly feels good to be back again.*

Fade out.

Fade in to a flag waving from a mast. Music. The word SYLVANIA appears over it, then we wipe to a shot of Sylvania itself. It is another Ruritanian town, of more southern aspect than Freedonia.

The music ends as a diagonal wipe transports us to TRENTINO's office. TRENTINO is seated at his desk in close-up, holding a newspaper.

AGITATOR off: *I have failed, Ambassador.*

TRENTINO: *I know it, I know it, you idiot!*

Close-up of the AGITATOR, leaning over TRENTINO's desk with a cringing expression.

AGITATOR: *I'm sorry.*

TRENTIONO off: *You have muddled everything.*

We now see him at his desk in the foreground, with the AGITATOR beyond him.

TRENTINO: *If you'd started the revolution as I planned, during the turmoil I could have stepped in and placed Freedonia under the Sylvanian flag — our flag.*

Close-up of the AGITATOR, leaning over the desk.

AGITATOR: *But Firefly blocked us. Your Excellency . . .*

Resume on TRENTINO from his point of view.

111

AGITATOR off : . . . *you have no idea how popular he is in Freedonia.*
TRENTINO : *Oh, yes, I've known of that too. That's why I have two spies shadowing him. I want to find out something about him — something to disgrace him, to discredit him with the people.*

He turns as the door opens off-screen and we cut to TRENTINO'S SECRETARY, who has come in through the door.

SECRETARY : *Ambassador, Chicolini and Pinky are here.*

Resume on TRENTINO at his desk, with the AGITATOR in back view.

TRENTINO : *Ah, those are my two spies. Show them in.* To the AGITATOR : *Wait outside.*

The AGITATOR hurries off in the background and we cut back to the SECRETARY as she opens the door, revealing PINKY in disguise.

We see CHICOLINI and PINKY standing in the doorway, both wearing bearded masks and hats. The eyes on PINKY'S mask whirl round. CHICOLINI removes his mask and grins, then spins PINKY round to reveal his face on the other side.

CHICOLINI : *We fool you good, heh?*

Shot of TRENTINO.

TRENTINO genially : *Gentlemen!* He starts forward.

Resume on the door, which the SECRETARY is holding open. TRENTINO advances towards CHICOLINI and PINKY with open arms, but they suddenly dive past him to the desk as a bell rings.

At the desk, PINKY answers first one phone, then the other, but the bell goes on ringing.

TRENTINO : *Gentlemen, what is this?*

A closer shot excludes him as CHICOLINI replies :

CHICOLINI : *Sssh! This is spy stuff!*

PINKY listens to both phones at once but the bell still goes on ringing. Finally he gives a grin and pulls a large alarm clock out of his pocket. CHICOLINI laughs.

SECRETARY off : *A telegram for you sir.*

As she finishes, we see her and TRENTINO.

TRENTINO : *Oh!*

CHICOLINI and PINKY rush round beside him. PINKY grabs the telegram, looks at it, then screws it up and throws it on the floor in a rage.

113

CHICOLINI : *He gets mad because he can't read.*

The SECRETARY exits and PINKY leers after her.

TRENTINO : *Oh, I see. Well, gentlemen, we have serious matters to discuss.*

Camera pans with them to the desk, then cuts to show them from a high angle.

TRENTINO : *So please be seated.*

CHICOLINI and PINKY slide under TRENTINO as he sits down. PINKY whistles while CHICOLINI sings :

CHICOLINI : *Rock-a-bye . . .*

In a medium shot of the group, PINKY continues to whistle and puts his feet up on the desk while the other two get up again.

TRENTINO : *Gentlemen! Gentlemen! Now, about that information I asked you to get.*

CHICOLINI reaches in his pocket.

CHICOLINI : *Wait, wait, wait, wait. Here, have a cigar.*

We see his hands as he holds out the charred butt of a cigar. TRENTINO's hand takes it from him.

Seen from below TRENTINO looks at the butt with distaste.

114

CHICOLINI off : *That's a good quarter cigar.*
Back to the group.
CHICOLINI : *I smoked the other three-quarters myself.*
TRENTINO : *Yes. Well, no thank you. I have one of my own.*
He throws down the butt and produces a cigar from a box on
the desk. PINKY leaps up and grabs it in his mouth.
TRENTINO : *Here, try one of these.*
Shot of PINKY and CHICOLINI. PINKY tries to light the cigar
with the telephone receiver.
CHICOLINI : *Aw, 'at'sa no good.*
He takes out a lighter but finds that it does not work.
Resume on all three of them as PINKY pulls a blowlamp out
of his pocket. It ignites with a roar, and he lights his own
cigar, then TRENTINO'S.
CHICOLINI : *'At'sa good, all right. 'At'sa fine. 'At'sa good.*
PINKY blows out the flame.
In another shot of the group camera pans, excluding CHICOLINI,
while PINKY puts the blowlamp down on the desk behind
TRENTINO. The Sylvanian ambassador turns to CHICOLINI,
holding his cigar behind his back.
TRENTINO : *Now, let's concentrate. Have you been trailing Firefly?*
PINKY opens a drawer in the desk and snips the end off
TRENTINO'S cigar with a pair of scissors; it falls into the drawer.
Camera pans to include CHICOLINI again.
CHICOLINI laughing : *Have we been trailing Firefly? Why, my
partner — he's got a nose just like a bloodhound.*
TRENTINO turning to look at PINKY : *Really?*
CHICOLINI : *Yeah, and the rest of his face don't look so good either.*
The three of them are seen standing in a row behind the desk.
TRENTINO tries to puff on his truncated cigar, then looks
suspiciously at PINKY.
CHICOLINI : *Look. We find out all about this Firefly.* He pulls out
a letter. *Here, look at this.*
TRENTINO grabs it and sits down.
TRENTINO : *Ah very good, very good. Wait a minute. We must not
be disturbed.*
Close-up of his hand pressing a buzzer on the desk.
The trio are seen from the side as the SECRETARY enters in the
background and comes up to the desk.

115

SECRETARY : *Yes, sir?*
TRENTINO : *Oh . . . This is a very important conference, and I do
not wish to be interrupted.*
Shot of TRENTINO, PINKY and the SECRETARY.
SECRETARY : *Yes sir.*
She sees PINKY leering at her and backs away nervously. PINKY
starts to follow, but CHICOLINI restrains him.
CHICOLINI off : *Ah-ah! Ah-ha!* He snaps his fingers.
Resume on the three of them beyond the desk. TRENTINO gets
up in exasperation.
TRENTINO : *Gentlemen, we are not getting anywhere.* He puts his
cigar in the ashtray.
Close-up of PINKY's hand as he balances the cigar on the end
of the buzzer board.
PINKY hits the cigar in the air with a ruler and belts it across
the room.
We see the others as PINKY runs to first base by the door, then
back to the desk. He throws himself down on the carpet and
CHICOLINI stands over him.

116

CHICOLINI : *You're out!*

He goes back to the other side of TRENTINO. PINKY tries to press the buzzer, but TRENTINO raises a finger.

TRENTINO to PINKY : *Ah-ah-ah!* To both of them : *Now, gentlemen, please! Will you tell me what you found out about Firefly?*

Shot of him and CHICOLINI.

CHICOLINI : *Well, you remember you gave us a picture of a man and said follow him?*

TRENTINO : *Oh, yes.*

CHICOLINI : *Well, we get on the job right away . . .* He gestures dramatically *. . . and in one hour . . . even in less than one hour . . .*

TRENTINO excitedly : *Yes?*

CHICOLINI : *. . . we lose-a da picsh . . .* TRENTINO sighs *. . . Dat'sa pretty quick work, huh?*

TRENTINO : *But I asked you to dig up something I can use against Firefly. Did you bring me his record?*

Resume on the three. PINKY gets out a gramophone record from under his coat and hands it to TRENTINO. The ambassador gets up, at his wits' end.

TRENTINO : *No, no!*

He throws the record over his shoulder. PINKY pulls out a gun. We see the record flying through the air. A shot rings out and it disintegrates.

Back to the group as CHICOLINI rings a handbell which he has found on the desk and hands PINKY a cigar from the box.

CHICOLINI : *And da boy gets a cigar.*

He slams the lid on TRENTINO's fingers.

TRENTINO : *Oww!* He shakes his fingers; PINKY commiserates. *Now, Chicolini . . .*

Shot of CHICOLINI and TRENTINO. TRENTINO sits down.

TRENTINO wagging a finger : *. . . I want a full detailed report of your investigation.*

PINKY is partly visible to the right.

CHICOLINI : *All right, I tell you. Monday we watch Firefly's house. but he no come out. He wasn't home. Tuesday we go to the ball game, but he fool us. He no show up. Wednesday he go to the ball game, and we fool him. We no show up. Thursday was a double header. Nobody show up. Friday it rained all day. There was no ball game so we stayed home and we listened to it over the radio.*

TRENTINO exasperated: *Then you didn't shadow Firefly?*
CHICOLINI: *Oh, sure we shadow Firefly. We shadow him all day.*
TRENTINO: *But what day was that?*
CHICOLINI: *Shadderday.*

Cut to include PINKY. TRENTINO clutches his head in his hands.
CHICOLINI laughing: *'At'sa some joke, eh, Boss?*

PINKY snips at TRENTINO's hair, which is standing up between his fingers.

Resume on TRENTINO and CHICOLINI.
TRENTINO: *Now, will you tell be what happened on Saturday?*
CHICOLINI: *I'm glad you asked me. We follow this man down to a roadhouse and at this roadhouse he meet a married lady.*
TRENTINO: *A married lady?*
CHICOLINI: *Yeah. I think it was his wife.*
TRENTINO: *Firefly has no wife.*
CHICOLINI: *No?*
TRENTINO: *No.*
CHICOLINI: *Den you know what I think, Boss?*
TRENTINO: *What?*
CHICOLINI: *I think we follow da wrong man.*

We see the three of them again, facing camera. TRENTINO gets up.
TRENTINO: *Oh, gentlemen, I am disappointed.* They hang their heads. *I entrusted you with a mission of great importance . . .* They look up eagerly . . . *and you failed.* They hang their heads again. *However . . .* They look up again . . . *I am going to give you one more chance.*

A closer shot of the three of them, from the side. TRENTINO bends over, looking in a drawer, and PINKY cuts off his coat tails.
TRENTINO: *I have credentials here that will get you into any place in Freedonia. If I can only . . . Ah, here we are.*

He straightens up and hands CHICOLINI a document.
Shot of TRENTINO and PINKY.
TRENTINO: *Now, are you sure that you can trap Firefly?*

PINKY nods and pulls out a mousetrap.
We see PINKY's hands with the mousetrap. It snaps shut.
Back to TRENTINO and PINKY. TRENTINO sighs in despair.
We see the three of them from the side again. TRENTINO

118

turns towards CHICOLINI in the background, while PINKY picks
up a paste pot.

TRENTINO : *Remember, this time . . .*

PINKY's hand dips the brush in the paste.

TRENTINO off : *. . . I expect results.*

Resume on the group as TRENTINO bends over, shaking hands
with CHICOLINI.

TRENTINO : *Goodbye, and good luck.*

PINKY smears paste on the seat of TRENTINO's trousers.

CHICOLINI : *Okay, Cap. Come on, Pinky.*

He goes off, while PINKY waves to TRENTINO.

Another shot looking towards the door. TRENTINO sits on the
desk with his hand outstretched.

TRENTINO : *Goodbye.*

PINKY shakes his hand and exits, leaving TRENTINO's fingers
caught in the mousetrap. TRENTINO gets up with an agonised
expression — and the newspaper stuck to his backside. He
groans and tries to remove his fingers from the trap. Fade out.

Fade in to a sign on a door which reads :

FREEDONIA CHAMBER OF DEPUTIES
In Conference — Do not disturb under any *circumstances.*

A ball is heard bouncing off-screen.

Dissolve to the interior of the Chamber of Deputies, where FIREFLY is standing at his desk at the end of the council table, playing ' jacks '. BOB is sitting beside him.

Dissolve to show the council table from above. The ministers watch transfixed on either side while FIREFLY plays at the far end. He misses the ball and throws the jacks on the floor. Camera tracks in.

FIREFLY : *All right, the meeting is called to order.*

He bangs a gavel on the table and the MINISTER OF FINANCE gets up.

MINISTER OF FINANCE : *Your Excellency, here is the Treasury Department's report.* He hands it up to FIREFLY. *I hope you'll find it clear.*

FIREFLY : *Clear? Huh! Why, a four-year-old child could understand this report.*

Shot of him and BOB.

FIREFLY : *Run out and find me a four-year-old child. I can't make head or tail out of it.* He hands the report to BOB.

Seen from the end of the table, the ministers look towards FIREFLY in the background.

FIREFLY : *And now, members of the Cabinet . . .* He bangs the gavel *. . . we'll take up old business.*

The MINISTER OF COMMERCE gets up.

MINISTER OF COMMERCE : *I wish to discuss the tariff.*

FIREFLY : *Sit down. That's new business. No old business? Very well . . .* He bangs the gavel *. . . then we'll take up new business.*

The MINISTER OF COMMERCE gets up again.

MINISTER OF COMMERCE : *Now, about that tariff.*

FIREFLY and BOB are seen from above, with the ministers in the foreground.

FIREFLY : *Too late. That's old business already. Sit down.*

The MINISTER OF WAR gets up.

MINISTER OF WAR : *Gentlemen, as your Secretary of War, I . . .*

FIREFLY : *The Secretary of War is out of order . . .*

A closer shot of FIREFLY and BOB.

FIREFLY: *Which reminds me, so is the plumbing.* To BOB: *Make a note of that . . . Never mind, I'll do it myself.*

He picks up a long, wavy quill and starts to write.

MINISTER OF LABOUR off: *The Department of Labour wishes to report that . . .*

Cut to include the ministers again.

MINISTER OF LABOUR standing: *. . . the workers of Freedonia are demanding shorter hours.*

FIREFLY: *Very well, we'll give them shorter hours. We'll start by cutting their lunch hour to twenty minutes. And now, gentlemen, we've got to start looking for a new Treasurer.*

The MINISTER OF LABOUR sits down, bewildered.

ANOTHER MINISTER getting up: *But you appointed one last week.*

FIREFLY: *That's the one I'm looking for.*

A reverse shot down the table shows the ministers facing camera.

MINISTER OF WAR rising: *Gentlemen! Gentlemen! Enough of this. How about taking up the tax?*

Resume on FIREFLY and BOB.

FIREFLY removing his cigar: *How about taking up the carpet?* He puts his feet up on the desk.

We see the MINISTER OF WAR again, standing, with some other ministers sitting behind.

MINISTER OF WAR: *I still insist we must take up the tax.*

Back to FIREFLY and BOB.

FIREFLY leaning towards BOB: *He's right. You've got to take up the tacks before you take up the carpet.*

The minister are seen from a high angle.

MINISTER OF WAR: *I give all my time and energy to my duties and what do I get?*

Close-up of FIREFLY.

FIREFLY: *You get awfully tiresome after a while.*

A closer shot of the MINISTER OF WAR.

MINISTER OF WAR: *Sir, you try my patience!*

Back to FIREFLY and BOB. FIREFLY gets up and leans forward.

FIREFLY: *I don't mind if you do. You must come over and try mine some time.*

We see the MINISTER OF WAR again.

MINISTER OF WAR waving his arms: *That's the last straw! I resign. I wash my hands of the whole business.*

In a shot of the scene, the MINISTER OF WAR exits in indignation.

FIREFLY: *A good idea. You can wash your neck, too.*

Fade out.

Fade in to the street outside the Chamber of Deputies, where CHICOLINI is seen by a peanut stand on a barrow.

CHICOLINI: *Peanuts!*

PINKY enters from the left, and we cut to medium close-up as he comes up behind the cart and starts stuffing his pockets full of peanuts. CHICOLINI turns to face camera, daubing mustard on a frankfurter.

As CHICOLINI is about to put the frankfurter in his mouth, PINKY snips the end off with his scissors.

CHICOLINI throws away the frankfurter in disgust, seen in the medium close-up again.

CHICOLINI: *Hey, come here.* He pushes PINKY.

Shot of the scene.

CHICOLINI: *Just the guy I want to see. What do you find out about this guy, Firefly? You find outa something? You no find out something? You spy on him? You no spy on him?*

PINKY gives him his leg. CHICOLINI thrusts it aside, then we cut in on the two of them.

CHICOLINI: *What'sa matter? All the time I talk to you, you no say nothin'. What'sa matter you no speak?* PINKY puts a peanut in his mouth. He crunches the shell and splutters: *Stop it! Whata you find? Eh? Whata you find?* PINKY produces a handful of peanuts; CHICOLINI knocks them out of his hand. *'At'sa no good.*

A longer shot includes a LEMONADE VENDOR standing by his cart on the right.

CHICOLINI pushing PINKY: *Hey, come here. You acta crazy, what'sa matter for you? What you make da face like this?* He grabs PINKY's face and shakes it. *What'sa matter for you?*

PINKY gets angry. In a closer shot of the group, he aims at CHICOLINI with one fist and starts swinging the other.

CHICOLINI: *Aw, come on, you wanna fight? You wanna fight?*

Come on, I give you fight.

Back to the scene as the VENDOR watches between the other two while CHICOLINI swings back his fist.

CHICOLINI : *Come on. I give you fight. Come on.*

PINKY kicks him in the pants, and we cut back to the closer shot again.

CHICOLINI angry : *Hey, upstairs this time, no downstairs.*

PINKY takes aim and starts swinging his fist again.

Resume on the scene as the VENDOR turns to serve a customer in the background.

CHICOLINI : *Come on.*

PINKY kicks him in the pants again. CHICOLINI pushes him angrily back into the customer.

CHICOLINI : *What you think you gonna do, eh?*

PINKY thrusts his hand into the customer's pocket.

A closer shot excludes CHICOLINI as the customer turns in amazement, then wrestles free and goes off leaving PINKY with his handkerchief. He comes back and grabs the handkerchief, then goes off again indignantly. The VENDOR, who

has been watching curiously, now finds PINKY's hand in his pocket. He slaps the hand away as CHICOLINI appears in the background.

Back to the scene again.

VENDOR angrily : *Hey, what's the idea of fightin' in front of my place and driving my customers away?*

PINKY sits down on the wheel of the VENDOR's cart.

CHICOLINI : *Hey, mister, you got a mistake some place. I no fight.* Seen in a closer shot again, PINKY produces his scissors and snips off the VENDOR's pocket which is still hanging out of his trousers. The VENDOR does not notice.

CHICOLINI : *You understand? This guy he'sa working for me. I ask him something and he no tell me nothing. I ask him why he no speak, and alla time he no speak.*

PINKY starts happily filling the amputated pocket with peanuts.

CHICOLINI : *And what do you think he do? He make a fight and go like-a dis.* He kicks the VENDOR in the pants.

Camera pans, excluding PINKY.

VENDOR : *Hey, what's the idea?*

CHICOLINI : *Aw, 'at'sa not my idea, 'at's his idea. Alla time he say nothing. Every time I speak . . .*

VENDOR : *Will you shut up?*

Resume on the group. The VENDOR turns back to PINKY.

VENDOR : *Say, listen, what are you doing around here?*

PINKY leans against him, sounding one of the horns which is stuck in his belt.

Shot of PINKY and the VENDOR.

VENDOR pushing him away : *Who are you?*

PINKY leans against him again. Sound of horn.

VENDOR : *Hey, can't you say . . .*

Two horns sound.

VENDOR pushing him away : *Can't you say anything?*

Back to the group.

CHICOLINI : *No, he no say nothin'. He . . .*

VENDOR : *Aw, shut up!*

CHICOLINI : *I am shut up, but Mister . . .*

A closer shot of all three.

CHICOLINI : *. . . you no understand. Look, he's a spy and I'm a spy. He works for me. I want him to find out something, but he no* *find out what I want to find out . . .*

The VENDOR runs his hand wearily over his face.

CHICOLINI: *Now, how am I gonna find out what I want to find out if he don't find out what I gotta find out?*

VENDOR desperate: *Will you quit annoying me?*

CHICOLINI: *All right, I quit.*

Shot of the scene.

CHICOLINI: *All you gotta do is to make him stop doing this.*

He kicks the VENDOR in the pants.

VENDOR: *Ugh! Ohhh!*

He clutches the air behind him and PINKY gives him his leg.

We see the three of them in medium close-up.

VENDOR advancing on PINKY: *Now, just for that I'm gonna tear you limb from limb, limb . . . Ugh!*

He advances on PINKY, hands clawing the air; PINKY grabs his hand and starts shaking it violently, grinning from ear to ear. Both their hats fall off.

Back to the scene as they both bend down and reach for their hats. The VENDOR grunts.

125

They put on their hats and the VENDOR turns grimly to
CHICOLINI, saying:

VENDOR: *In fact I'll do the same . . .*

CHICOLINI points dumbly at the grinning PINKY — they have
on the wrong hats. The VENDOR takes off PINKY's hat with a
sigh, hands it to PINKY and reaches for his own. PINKY drops
it on the ground.

Resume on the scene: PINKY and CHICOLINI watch as the
VENDOR bends to pick up his hat. Then we cut back to the
closer shot again.

VENDOR: *Ohhh!*

As CHICOLINI addresses him, the VENDOR puts on his hat;
PINKY, standing behind him, swaps it neatly for his own,
which he puts on the VENDOR's head.

CHICOLINI: *Now, you see, I no say one thing, Mister, before when
you . . .*

VENDOR: *No!* . . . He breathes heavily, and clutches the air
desperately.

CHICOLINI: *No, I no say . . .*

The VENDOR's groping hand finds PINKY's leg again; he
thrusts aside the leg, whips off his hat in a rage and finds it's
the wrong one.

VENDOR: *Doh!*

He throws down the hat and reaches for his own; PINKY takes
it off and throws it on the ground.

In another medium shot, the VENDOR bends down to retrieve
his hat; PINKY kicks it across to CHICOLINI. The VENDOR goes
after it and CHICOLINI kicks it back to PINKY, who picks it up.
PINKY brushes off the hat with an indigant expression.

Resume on the scene. PINKY holds out the hat and the VENDOR
reaches for it. PINKY drops it on an elastic and it goes up and
down like a yoyo. Breathing heavily, the VENDOR reaches for
the hat again and catches it. PINKY puts his foot in the hat
as it hangs from the VENDOR's hand. The VENDOR whips it
away but PINKY knocks it to the ground again. CHICOLINI picks
it up and puts it on top of his own, while the VENDOR reaches
for PINKY, who makes a 'pax' sign with both hands. The
VENDOR bends down for his hat, can't find it, mops his brow,
then finds it's on CHICOLINI. PINKY puts on his own hat.

126

In a closer shot again the VENDOR grabs his hat from CHICOLINI and puts it on with CHICOLINI's underneath. PINKY gives CHICOLINI his hat and takes the VENDOR's, leaving the VENDOR with CHICOLINI's. The VENDOR, who has not noticed this last manoeuvre, looks from PINKY to CHICOLINI in bewilderment. PINKY makes a crease in the VENDOR's hat, puts it on again, and sticks out his tongue, goggle-eyed. The VENDOR turns back to him and gets a fright.

Back to the scene as the hat business continues. The hats get passed round and round until the VENDOR ends up with his own. He then finds he's holding PINKY's leg, then CHICOLINI's.

VENDOR spluttering : *Aw now, now, I'm goin' to get you . . .*

He chases CHICOLINI off while PINKY pulls out his horn.

PINKY is seen siphoning lemonade into the horn from the vat on the VENDOR's cart, then we cut to a longer shot as he puts the horn back in his belt. The VENDOR reappears.

VENDOR : *What are you doin'?*

Seen in the closer shot, PINKY leans against the VENDOR and the horn squirts lemonade in his face.

VENDOR : *Aw!*

Another shot of the two of them.

VENDOR going for PINKY : *Why, you . . .*

PINKY leans against him again. Sound of the horn. The VENDOR splutters in the shower of lemonade, then starts roaring with laughter.

Back to the scene as PINKY joins in, shaking with silent laughter, then cut back to the two of them. While PINKY laughs with his head thrown back, the VENDOR grabs the horn and squirts lemonade down inside his trousers. He goes off as the smile freezes on PINKY's face.

PINKY shifts uncomfortably from one leg to the other, then goes off whistling, with a pained expression.

We now see CHICOLINI by the peanut stand, as the VENDOR rushes up to him.

VENDOR : *I'll teach you to kick me!*

CHICOLINI : *You don't have to teach me. I know how.*

He kicks the VENDOR, whose hat flies off. PINKY enters from the right and catches it.

VENDOR : *Ohhh!*

127

He grabs CHICOLINI and shakes him, while PINKY puts his hat over the flame in the warming cabinet on the peanut cart.
Shot of PINKY and the hat as it bursts into flames. Camera pans to include the VENDOR, who is throttling CHICOLINI.
CHICOLINI off : *Stop it now. Look out!*
PINKY whistles and taps the VENDOR on the back; he turns and sees the hat.
Shot of the scene. The VENDOR runs his hands over his head and groans, while PINKY points at the burning hat, grinning.
CHICOLINI : *Oh, 'at'sa good, eh?*
Fade out.

Fade in to the same street from a low angle, with CHICOLINI and his peanut stand. Two girls pass across the scene.
CHICOLINI shouting : *Peanuts!*
FIREFLY appears on the balcony in the background.
FIREFLY : *Hey!*
CHICOLINI throws him up a bag of peanuts, and we cut to a low angle shot of him leaning on the balcony.
FIREFLY : *Do you want to be a public nuisance?*
Reverse shot of CHICOLINI from FIREFLY's point of view.
CHICOLINI looking up : *Sure. How much does the job pay?*
Back to FIREFLY.
FIREFLY : *I've got a good mind to join a club and beat you over the head with it.*
Resume on CHICOLINI.
CHICOLINI shouting : *Peanuts . . . to you!*
Camera on FIREFLY again.
FIREFLY : *Have you got a license?*
CHICOLINI : *License? . . .*
Resume on him; he points to a dog sitting on the ground behind him.
CHICOLINI : *No, but my dog — he'sa got millions of 'em. Believe me, he's some smart dog. You know, he went with Admiral Byrd to the pole?*
Another shot of FIREFLY.
FIREFLY : *I'll bet the dog got to the pole first.*
Back to CHICOLINI.
CHICOLINI : *You win!*

128

FIREFLY beckons.

FIREFLY : *Come on up here. I want to scare the Cabinet.*

In a long shot of the scene, FIREFLY leaves the balcony.

Dissolve to the interior of the Chamber of Deputies, where FIREFLY and CHICOLINI approach the former's desk from either side as a phone rings. CHICOLINI rushes to answer it.

CHICOLINI : *Hello. No. No. No, he's not in. All right, I'll tell him. Goodbye.*

The two of them are seen in medium close-up.

FIREFLY shelling a peanut : *I'm sorry I'm not in. I wanted to have a long talk with you.* He sits down. *Now listen here. You give up that silly peanut stand and I'll get you a soft government job. Now, let's see . . .*

A longer shot of the two of them.

FIREFLY getting up again : *How would you like a job in the mint?*

CHICOLINI reflecting : *Mint? No, no, I no like-a mint. Uh . . . what other flavour you got?*

The phone rings and CHICOLINI beats FIREFLY to it again.

CHICOLINI : *Hello, hello.*

They are seen in a closer shot.

CHICOLINI into the phone : *No, not yet. All right, I tell him. Goodbye, thank you.* To FIREFLY : *That was for you again.*

FIREFLY : *I wonder whatever became of me . . .*

Shot of the scene as FIREFLY searches round the desk.

FIREFLY : *I should have been back here a long time ago. Now, listen here. I've got a swell job for you . . .* He climbs onto his presidential chair . . . *but first I'll have to ask you a couple of . . .*

Back to medium close-up.

FIREFLY : *. . . important questions.* He perches on the back of the chair. *Now, what is it that has four pairs of pants, lives in Philadelphia, and it never rains but it pours?* He leers at camera.

CHICOLINI : *'At'sa good one. I give you three guesses.*

FIREFLY : *Now lemme see. Has four pair of pants, lives in Philadelphia. Is it male or female?*

CHICOLINI : *No I don't think so.*

FIREFLY : *Is he dead?*

CHICOLINI : *Who?*

FIREFLY : *I don't know. I give up.*

He gets down from the chair, puffing on his cigar.

CHICOLINI: *I give up, too. Now, I ask you another one. What is it got a big black moustache, smokes a big black cigar and is a big pain in the neck?*

FIREFLY: *Now, don't tell me.* Pondering: *Has a big black moustache, smokes a big black cigar and is a big pain in the ...*

The penny drops.

CHICOLINI: *Uh ...*

FIREFLY turning to CHICOLINI: *Does he wear glasses?*

CHICOLINI laughing: *'At'sa right. You guess it quick.*

FIREFLY: *Just for that you don't get the job I was going to give you.*

CHICOLINI: *What job?*

FIREFLY: *Secretary of War.*

CHICOLINI: *All right, I take it.*

FIREFLY: *Sold!*

They shake hands. At that moment the phone rings again.

Shot of the scene as they both dive for the phone. PINKY enters in the background and beats them to it.

In a closer shot of the three of them, PINKY answers the phone and carries on a conversation, using his horns. He asks a question.

Cut to exclude the others. PINKY shakes his head, asks another question, laughs, then growls and slams down the phone indignantly.

Resume on the group as PINKY whistles and gestures to FIREFLY, indicating the call was for him.

FIREFLY: *You know, I'd be lost without a telephone.*

PINKY gestures as if to say ' Don't mention it ', and turns to go, but FIREFLY stops him.

FIREFLY: *Hey, don't go away. I want to talk to you.* To CHICOLINI: *Now, where were we? Oh, yes.* Camera pans as he conducts CHICOLINI to the door. *Now that you're Secretary of War, what kind of an army do you think we ought to have?*

We see the two of them at the door.

CHICOLINI: *Well, I tell you what I think. I think we should have a standing army.*

Resume on PINKY. He sits at FIREFLY's desk and starts writing with the quill. The long plume tickles his nose.

Firefly off : *Why should we have a standing army?*
Resume on him and Chicolini.
Chicolini : Because we then save money on chairs.
Firefly exits with Chicolini and boots him downstairs, off-screen; there is a loud crash; Firefly reappears.
Fireplay : *Peanuts!*
Camera tracks with him as he comes back to Pinky, humming, and we cut in on the two of them.
Firefly : *Scat!*
He takes Pinky's *place at the desk and starts writing.* Pinky snips the top off the plume with his scissors.
Firefly looking up : *Say, who are you, anyway?*
Pinky pulls up his coat sleeve, and we see . . .
Pinky's face tattooed on his arm.
Resume on Pinky on Firefly.
Firefly : *I don't go in much for modern art. Have you got anything by one of the old masters?*
Pinky pulls up his other sleeve; oriental music is heard.
Close-up of a girl tattooed on his arm. She does a belly dance in time to the music as Pinky flexes his muscles.
Firefly off : *Not bad!*
The music stops, and we resume on Pinky and Firefly.
Firefly : *You don't happen to have her telephone number?*
Pinky drops his collection of horns and pulls up his shirt. Firefly copies the number off Pinky's side, seen in a medium shot.
Firefly : *Say, you could be a big help to me. Where do you live?*
Pinky starts to pull open his shirt.
A closer shot of the two of them as Pinky displays a picture of a dog kennel tattooed on his chest. Firefly leans forward to look.
Firefly : *Well, it's not much of a place, but it's home.* Pinky beckons him closer, and he leans forward and says : *Meow!*
A dog's head appears at the kennel door, seen in close-up, and barks loudly.
Resume on Pinky and Firefly, who leaps back in alarm.
Firefly recovering : *Well, I know one thing. I bet you haven't got a picture of my grandfather.*
Pinky takes off his coat, bends over and starts to pull out

131

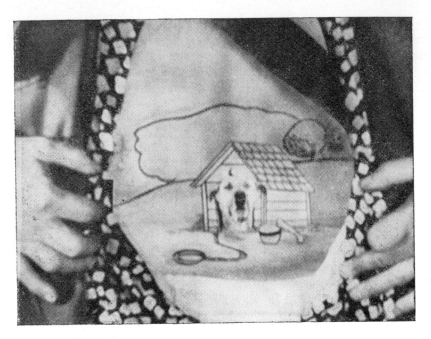

his shirt.

FIREFLY restraining him: *Ah-ah! Not now. Some other time.*

Seen in close-up, PINKY picks up his collection of horns. Camera pans with him to the door, where he exits with a merry wave.

We look towards the doorway as BOB enters, reaches up to take off his hat and finds it has been cut in half; he throws it out of the door. Camera pans as he moves across to FIREFLY.

BOB loudly: *Your Excellency.*

FIREFLY leaps up with a start and salutes, then bangs the gavel on his desk.

FIREFLY: *Quiet!*

Shot of him and BOB, who puts a letter on the desk.

BOB: *This letter is the work of Trentino. The man is trying to undermine you. Now, what are you going to do about it?*

FIREFLY picks up the letter.

FIREFLY: *I've got a good mind to ring his doorbell and run.*

BOB: *We've got to get rid of that man at once. Now, I've got a*

plan. You say something to make him mad, and he'll strike you . . .
He bangs his fist in his palm . . . *and we'll force him to leave the country.* He walks round behind FIREFLY's chair.
FIREFLY : *That's a swell plan. Why couldn't you arrange for me to strike him?*
We see the two of them facing one another across the chair.
BOB : *Ambassador Trentino is a very sensitive man. Perhaps if you insult him — he's a very easy man to insult. Why, I said something to Vera Marcal in his presence once and he slapped my face.*
FIREFLY : *Why didn't Vera slap your face?*
BOB : *She did.*
FIREFLY : *What'd you say to her?*
BOB leans forward and whispers in FIREFLY's ear. FIREFLY slaps his face.
FIREFLY : *You ought to be ashamed of yourself! Where did you hear that story?*
BOB : *Why, you told it to me.*
FIREFLY : *Oh, yes. I remember. I should have slapped Mrs Teasdale's face when she told it to me. Where is Trentino?*
BOB : *At Mrs Teasdale's tea party.*
FIREFLY : *Was I invited?*
BOB : *No.*
FIREFLY : *Take a letter.*
In a medium shot of the two of them, BOB sits at the desk while FIREFLY paces to and fro, dictating.
FIREFLY clearing his throat : '*You are cordially invited to attend my tea.*' *Er . . . sign Mrs Teasdale's name and tell her I accept. Come on, let's go.*
They make for the door.

Outside the palace, camera pans with PINKY as he drives up on the presidential motorcycle and halts at the bottom of the steps with a squeal of brakes.
A closer shot, with PINKY in the foreground. The trumpeters step forward in the background and sound a fanfare, as FIREFLY comes out of the palace and down the steps.
FIREFLY : *I've got an appointment to insult Ambassador Trentino and I don't want to keep him waiting. Step on it! . . .*
As he climbs into the sidecar, PINKY roars off on the motor-

cycle, leaving him standing.

FIREFLY chin on fist: *This is the fifth trip I've made today and I haven't been anywhere yet.*

Fade out.

Fade in to the grounds of MRS TEASDALE'S residence. Elegantly dressed guests are wandering to and fro. In the foreground, TRENTINO is sitting at a table with a sunshade. There is gay music as VERA approaches from the background, and we cut to a closer shot as she comes up some steps behind TRENTINO.

She sits down at the table.

VERA: *You don't seem to be making much progress with Mrs Teasdale, huh?*

TRENTINO despairing: *How can I? Every time I get her in the right mood to say 'Yes', Firefly pops in.*

VERA: *Well, this is your opportunity. He won't be here today.*

TRENTINO: *Are you sure?*

VERA: *Positive. I helped Mrs Teasdale with the . . . invitations.*

She makes the motions of tearing an invitation up and throwing it away.

TRENTINO: *Oh!*

We look towards the end of the garden as a LACKEY appears at the top of some steps.

LACKEY: *His Excellency . . .*

Shot of the lawn with the guests sitting at umbrella tables laid out on either side.

LACKEY off: *. . . Rufus T. Firefly!*

Music as the guests all rise and sing.

GUESTS: *Hail . . .*

FIREFLY appears at the end of the garden and comes past the lackey.

GUESTS singing, off: *. . . hail, Freedonia!*

Seen from above, FIREFLY passes one of the tables. He picks up a doughnut from a guest's plate and walks on, camera tracking ahead of him.

GUESTS singing: *Land of the brave . . .*

FIREFLY'S hand dunks the doughnut in someone's coffee.

GUESTS singing off: *. . . and . . .*

134

Resume on FIREFLY and the guests. Camera tracks on again as he walks forward, eating the doughnut.

GUESTS singing : . . . *free!*

The music ends.

We now see TRENTINO, seated alone with MRS TEASDALE in a corner of the garden.

Resume on the guests as FIREFLY goes off in the foreground.

TRENTINO meanwhile clasps MRS TEASDALE's hand and says :

TRENTINO : *Gloria, I've waited for years. I can't be put off any longer. I love you! I want you! Can't you see I'm at your feet?*

He goes down on one knee.

They are seen in a medium shot as FIREFLY enters behind TRENTINO.

FIREFLY : *When you get through with her feet, you can start on mine!*

TRENTINO turns with a sigh, and we cut in on the group.

FIREFLY : *If that isn't an insult, I don't know what is! Gloria, I love you!*

He dives for MRS TEASDALE, knocking TRENTINO out of the way.

In a closer shot, FIREFLY pushes TRENTINO off and kneels at MRS TEASDALE's feet.

FIREFLY : *I realize how lonely you are . . .*

Cut to include TRENTINO again.

TRENTINO to MRS TEASDALE : *Can't we go some place where we can be by ourselves?*

FIREFLY pointing at TRENTINO : *What can this mug offer you? Wealth and family?*

Resume on just the two of them.

FIREFLY : *I can't give you wealth, but — uh — we can have a little family of our own.*

MRS TEASDALE melting : *Oh, Rufus!*

FIREFLY : *All I can offer you is a roofus over your head.*

MRS TEASDALE : *Your Excellency, I really don't know what to say.*

FIREFLY : *I wouldn't know what to say either if I was in your place.*

We see TRENTINO again as FIREFLY turns towards him.

FIREFLY : *Maybe you can suggest something. As a matter of fact,*

135

you do suggest something. He stands on the bench. *To me you suggest a baboon.*

TRENTINO : *What?*

The group is seen from below.

FIREFLY standing over TRENTINO : *I . . . I'm sorry I said that. It isn't fair to the rest of the baboons.*

TRENTINO furious : *This man's conduct is inexcusable. Why I'll . . .*

MRS TEASDALE : *Oh, gentlemen, gentlemen!*

TRENTINO : *I did not come here to be insulted!*

He starts out and FIREFLY goes after him.

MRS TEASDALE : *Oh!*

Camera tracks with TRENTINO as he strides across the garden, pursued by FIREFLY. The guests gather round in the background.

FIREFLY : *That's what you think!*

TRENTINO : *You swine!*

FIREFLY : *Come again?*

TRENTINO : *You worm!*

FIREFLY : *Once more?*

TRENTINO : *You upstart!*

MRS TEASDALE enters.

FIREFLY : *That's it!*

He slaps TRENTINO's face with his gloves; MRS TEASDALE gasps.

FIREFLY : *Touché!* He hands TRENTINO his card.

MRS TEASDALE : *Oh!*

TRENTINO tearing up the card : *Mrs Teasdale, I'm afraid this regrettable occurrence may plunge our countries into war.*

FIREFLY starts fencing with MRS TEASDALE's parasol.

MRS TEASDALE : *Oh, this is terrible!*

TRENTINO : *I've said enough. I'm a man of few words.*

FIREFLY : *I'm a man of one word. Scram!* TRENTINO exits. *The man doesn't live who can call a Firefly an upstart. Why, the Mayflower was full of Fireflys, and a few horseflies, too. The Fireflys were on the upper deck and the horseflies were on the Fireflys.* He kisses MRS TEASDALE's hand. *Good day, my sweet.*

He starts out, but she grabs him.

MRS TEASDALE : *Oh, your Excellency, I must speak to you!*

FIREFLY : *I'll see you at the theatre tonight. I'll hold your seat till*

you get there. After you get there, you're on your own.
LACKEY off : *His Excellency's car!*
FIREFLY shouting : *His Excellency's car.*
    He tucks MRS TEASDALE's parasol under his arm and goes
off.
    At the entrance to the garden, PINKY is on the motorcycle,
saluting; the motor is running. FIREFLY enters from the right.
Shot of the two of them as PINKY gestures FIREFLY into the
sidecar.
FIREFLY : *Oh, no, you don't! I'm not taking any more chances.
You can only fool a Firefly twice. This time you ride in the sidecar.*
    PINKY gets into the sidecar, grinning, while FIREFLY climbs
onto the motorcycle. The engine revs and he leans forward to
take the acceleration.
    Resume on the scene as PINKY roars off in the sidecar, leaving
the motorcycle standing.
    A reverse shot shows PINKY speeding up the drive, leaving
FIREFLY in the foreground; then we cut back to FIREFLY
leaning forward on the motorcycle. He sighs and says :

137

FIREFLY : *This is the only way to travel!*
  Fade out.

Fade in to the street where CHICOLINI has his peanut stand.
We see CHICOLINI and his dog, then PINKY enters in the
background.
CHICOLINI : *Hey, Pinky! Come here. Watch-a the stand.* To the
dog : *Come on Pastrom. Come on, come on.*
  He goes off with the dog, while the LEMONADE VENDOR comes
up and stands by the peanut cart; he is now wearing a straw
boater instead of the bowler he had earlier.
  Shot of PINKY and the VENDOR, who is eating peanuts. PINKY
holds his hand out for some; the VENDOR daubs it with
mustard, then goes on impassively eating. PINKY looks at his
hand in disgust, then grins and wipes it on the VENDOR's
sash. He cuts off the sash with his scissors, throws it aside, and
slaps the bag of peanuts from the VENDOR's hand. Unruffled,
the VENDOR picks up another bag from the stand and opens
it. PINKY begs for a nut; the VENDOR looks at him stonily.
PINKY looks up at the sky; the VENDOR does likewise, and
PINKY slaps the bag from his hand.
  Back to the scene : the VENDOR begins to get angry as PINKY
gathers an armful of peanut bags from the cart. He dashes
them to the ground, losing his hat, which PINKY hides behind
his back. The VENDOR bends down, searching on the ground,
and PINKY puts the hat on the flame in the glass cabinet.
Then he whistles and taps the VENDOR on the back.
  The VENDOR turns as PINKY whistles, and sees his hat in
flames.
VENDOR in despair : *Oooooooh!*
  Resume on the scene as he turns the peanut cart over with
a crash.
VENDOR : *Huh!*
  He exits, satisfied, dusting off his hands.
  We now see him at his lemonade stand, where a queue of
customers in Ruritanian dress are waiting to be served. As
he starts serving them with a ladle, PINKY comes up behind
him with his trousers rolled up, climbs into the vat of lemonade
and paddles in it gleefully with his bare feet. The customers

leave in disgust, watched by the bewildered VENDOR.
In a medium close-up, the VENDOR turns and sees the grinning
PINKY in the vat. He groans and clutches his head. Fade out.

Fade in to the drawing room of MRS TEASDALE's residence.
VERA is seated in an armchair with TRENTINO standing beside
her as MRS TEASDALE approaches from the background.

TRENTINO : *Mrs Teasdale.* He kisses her hand. *I deeply regret the
unfortunate affair with his Excellency, but his attitude left me no
alternative.*

VERA : *Maybe we can still avoid this terrible war.*

MRS TEASDALE : *Oh, if only we could!*

VERA : *Oh, yes . . .*

Cut to exclude her as she finishes.

VERA off : *. . . I'll do my best.*

MRS TEASDALE stands wringing her hands.

TRENTINO : *Er . . . Mrs Teasdale, I have been recalled by my
President.*

She turns to him in alarm.

MRS TEASDALE : *Then it is too late?*

TRENTINO : *Not if his Excellency will listen to reason. I am
prepared to pocket my pride and forget about the whole matter, if
he is.*

MRS TEASDALE : *Ambassador, that's wonderful of you, but I'm
afraid his Excellency won't hear of it.*

Shot of VERA.

VERA : *Oh, perhaps he will listen to you.*

Resume on all three.

MRS TEASDALE : *Do you think so?*

VERA : *Yes, of course.*

MRS TEASDALE : *I'll call him.* She starts off.

VERA : *Oh!*

We move to FIREFLY's bedroom, where camera shows some
crackers strewn on the bed, then pans along to FIREFLY, in
nightshirt and cap, lying in bed eating crackers. The telephone
rings and he lifts the receiver.

Back in MRS TEASDALE's drawing room, camera tracks in on
her as she speaks into the phone.

MRS TEASDALE : *I hate to disturb you. I know you're a very busy*

140

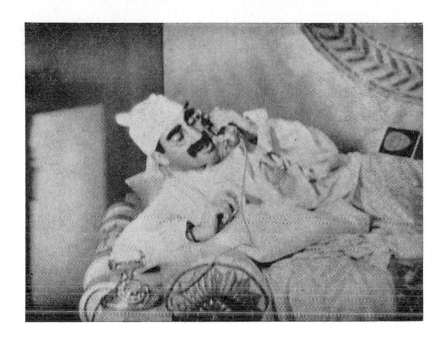

man, *but I must see you at once.*

Resume on FIREFLY.

FIREFLY : *Where are you? Oh! Why not come over here? You can come in the back way and no one'll see you.* A pause. *Well, if you think of it, bring some cheese.*

Back to MRS TEASDALE.

MRS TEASDALE : *But, your Excellency, you must come over. It's a long story. I can't tell it to you over the phone.*

FIREFLY replies.

FIREFLY : *Oh, it's that kind of a story! You ought to be ashamed of yourself. I'll be right over.* He hangs up.

Back in the drawing room, we see VERA and TRENTINO.

MRS TEASDALE off : *He'll be right over.* She enters. *Perhaps you'd better wait outside until I've had a chance to talk to him.*

TRENTINO : *Very well. We'll be out of here if you want us.*

MRS TEASDALE goes off, while TRENTINO takes VERA's arm and leads her towards the garden in the background.

Dissolve to the drawing room a little while later. MRS TEASDALE is pacing up and down in agitation. FIREFLY enters unnoticed and follows her up and down. Then he sits down in a chair, and camera tracks in as she turns and notices him.

MRS TEASDALE : *Oh!*

FIREFLY : *How'd you get in here?*

MRS TEASDALE standing over him : *Oh, your Excellency, I'm so sorry to have to disturb you. Will you ever forgive me?*

FIREFLY : *After I leave here tonight, will you ever forgive me?* He gets up and hands her an envelope. *Here are the plans of war.*

Shot of the two of them.

FIREFLY : *They're as valuable as your life, and that's putting 'em pretty cheap. Watch them like a cat watches her kittens. Have you ever had kittens? No, of course not. You're too busy running around playing bridge. Can't you see what I'm trying to tell you?* He puts his arms round her. *I love you. Why don't you marry me?*

MRS TEASDALE : *Why, marry you?*

FIREFLY : *You take me and I'll take a vacation. I'll need a vacation if we're going to get married.* They stand in a romantic pose, holding hands. *Married! I can see you right now in the kitchen, bending over a hot stove, but I can't see the stove. Come, come, say the word and you'll never see . . .*

Cut to medium shot as they sit down on the sofa.

FIREFLY : *. . . me again . . . Gloria!*

Then a closer shot as he puts his arms round her.

MRS TEASDALE with a happy smile : *Rufus, what are you thinking of?*

FIREFLY gazing into space : *Oh, I was just thinking of all the years I wasted collecting stamps.*

He draws her closer and she laughs.

We see them in medium close-up as FIREFLY sits forward and continues bashfully :

FIREFLY : *Oh . . . er . . . I suppose you'll think me a sentimental old fluff, but . . . er . . . would you mind giving me a lock of your hair?*

MRS TEASDALE : *A lock of my hair?* She laughs coyly. *Why, I had no idea . . .*

FIREFLY : *I'm letting you off easy. I was going to ask for the whole wig.*

We see VERA and TRENTINO coming in from the garden.

Then return to FIREFLY and MRS TEASDALE — FIREFLY is sitting on her lap. He sees the others approaching, rises and

142

strides off.

Resume on VERA and TRENTINO as FIREFLY comes up to them, followed by MRS TEASDALE.

FIREFLY : *So you've come to ask for clemency.*

MRS TEASDALE takes him aside.

MRS TEASDALE : *Your Excellency, the Ambassador's here on a friendly visit.*

A closer shot of the four of them.

MRS TEASDALE : *He's had a change of heart.*

FIREFLY : *A lot of good that'll do him. He's still got the same face.*

TRENTINO looks indignant and MRS TEASDALE sighs.

TRENTINO : *I'm sorry we lost our tempers. I'm willing to forget if you are.*

FIREFLY : *Forget? You ask me to forget? A Firefly never forgets. Why, my ancestors would rise from their graves and I would only have to bury them again. Nothing doing. I'm going back to clean the crackers out of my bed. I'm expecting company.*

In a longer shot of the group, he starts to leave, but MRS TEASDALE grabs him by the shoulder.

MRS TEASDALE : *Please wait!*

FIREFLY : *Let go of me, you bully!* He aims a mock punch at her.

MRS TEASDALE : *Oh!*

FIREFLY bows stiffly to TRENTINO, then we cut back to the closer shot.

TRENTINO arms folded : *I am willing to do anything to prevent this war.*

FIREFLY : *It's too late. I've already paid a month's rent on the battlefield.*

VERA comes round and lays a hand on his chest.

VERA : *Oh, your Excellency, isn't there something I can do?*

FIREFLY : *Yes, but I'll talk to you about that later.*

MRS TEASDALE : *Won't you reconsider? Please relent for my sake.*

FIREFLY : *Well, maybe I am a little headstrong, but I came by it honestly. My father was a little headstrong. My mother was a little Armstrong. The Headstrongs married the Armstrongs and that's why darkies were born. Heh!* He sits on the arm of a chair and continues jovially : *It was silly of me to lose my temper on account of that little thing you called me.*

The group are seen from another angle.

TRENTINO good naturedly: *Little thing I called you? Why, what did I call you?*

FIREFLY with a laugh: *Gosh, I don't even remember what it was.* They all laugh.

TRENTINO: *Well, do you mean worm?*

FIREFLY: *No, that wasn't it.*

TRENTINO: *I know. Swine.*

FIREFLY: *Huh-uh. No, it was a seven letter word.*

TRENTINO suddenly remembering: *Oh, yes. Upstart.*

FIREFLY: *That's it! Upstart!*

He gets up angrily and slaps TRENTINO with his glove.

MRS TEASDALE: *Oh, please, please!*

TRENTINO: *Mrs Teasdale, this man is impossible! This is an outrage. My course is clear. This means war!*

MRS TEASDALE: *Oh!*

TRENTINO: *You runt!*

FIREFLY: *I still like upstart the best.*

TRENTINO: *I shan't stay here a minute longer.*

FIREFLY: *Go, and never darken my towels again!*

MRS TEASDALE: *Oh!*

TRENTINO: *My hat!*

FIREFLY: *My towels!* He exits in the background.

MRS TEASDALE: *Oh!*

Fade out.

Fade in to TRENTINO's study. TRENTINO is surrounded by Sylvanian ministers and diplomats.

TRENTINO: *I happen to know that Freedonia's plans of war are in Mrs Teasdale's possession. I must get hold of them.*

AN ATTACHE: *Yes, but how?*

TRENTINO: *We have a week-end guest in Mrs Teasdale's house — Miss Marcal. Now, gentlemen, do you mind waiting for me outside? I'll join you in a moment.*

ATTACHE: *Certainly.*

They bow and exit, camera panning away from them as TRENTINO picks up the telephone.

In MRS TEASDALE's bedroom, MRS TEASDALE and VERA are sitting on the bed in night attire. The telephone rings off-screen.

144

Vera : *Excuse me.* She laughs nervously.

Camera tracks ahead of her as she comes into her bedroom and shuts her door, then sits down on the bed and answers the telephone.

Vera : *Hello. Yes, I am alone. No, not yet.*

We resume on Trentino, sitting at his desk.

Trentino into the telephone : *But Vera, we've got to work fast. You must get hold of those plans tonight. Chicolini and his partner should be there any minute. Do everything you can to help them.*

Back to Vera.

Vera : *But I must be very careful. There's another guest staying here for the week end — Firefly . . . I don't know. I think he's asleep.*

Outside Mrs Teasdale's house, Chicolini creeps into view, making for the front door. Chicolini beckons to Pinky who follows with a finger to his lips.

Seen in a closer shot they shush one another, and creep up to the front door.

At the door, Chicolini looks round nervously. Pinky makes a popping noise just behind him; Chicolini jumps with fright, scolds him, then says :

Chicolini : *Sssh! Ring the bell.*

Pinky pulls a large handbell from under his coat and rings it, shattering the silence.

Chicolini : *Sssh! Push the button.*

Pinky pokes his finger in Chicolini's navel.

In a longer shot, Chicolini pulls away and presses the buzzer on the door.

We now see a hedge in the foreground; Chicolini and Pinky hide behind it as the Butler comes out of the front door and looks from side to side. Pinky dives for the front door, followed by Chicolini, goes in and slams the door in Chicolini's face while the Butler looks behind the hedge. Chicolini hides behind the hedge again as the Butler goes back to the door, finds it shut and goes off to the left.

Cut to show Chicolini as he goes up to the door, rings the bell and hides behind the hedge again. Pinky comes out and looks over the hedge, whistling. Chicolini dives for the door behind him and slams the door in his face. Pinky presses the bell and hides.

We see Pinky hiding behind the hedge as Chicolini comes out again and looks over it. The Butler reappears in the background, goes in and shuts the door in the faces of Pinky and Chicolini.

As the two of them come back to the hedge, camera shows some French windows in the background. Vera comes out and beckons. They run towards her and all go into the house.

Seen from the interior, Vera, Pinky and Chicolini enter the darkened drawing room, then we cut to a closer shot of the group.

Chicolini : *You gotta da plans?*

Vera : *No, but they're somewheres in the house and you must find them. Oh, for Heaven's sakes, whatever you do, don't make a sound. If you're found, you're lost.*

Chicolini : *Oh, you crazy. How can I be lost if I'm found?*

Vera : *Ohhh!*

She looks anxiously round in the darkness and we cut to a medium close-up.

Vera to Pinky : *Got a flashlight?*

Pinky pulls his blowlamp from under his coat, and it lights with a roar. Vera exits.

Chicolini : *Sssh!*

Cut to include Vera again.

Vera : *You don't know how serious this is. If they catch you, you'll be court-martialled and shot.*

Pinky points an imaginary gun at his temple and fires.

Mrs Teasdale off : *Oh, Vera!*

Camera pans with Vera as she moves across to the piano. Chicolini follows her and hides by the piano keyboard.

Vera : *I must go before she looks for me. Now remember, whatever you do, don't make a sound.* She goes off.

We see Pinky by a clock standing against the wall. He pulls out his alarm clock, which says twelve o'clock, and sets the other clock to the same time. It starts to strike. Pinky puts a finger to his lips and moves on.

Camera follows Pinky as he moves past the piano. He sees a china duck on a table and stops.

The clock is still striking as Pinky picks up the duck — it

146

turns out to be a music box, which starts to play. PINKY puts a finger to his lips.

In a medium shot, he starts to dance like a mechanical doll, then plucks the strings of the piano, which play with the sound of a harp.

CHICOLINI hears the noise as he is going up the stairs. He stops and comes back down again, camera panning with him. We return to PINKY at the piano as CHICOLINI appears; the music continues loudly.

In a closer shot, CHICOLINI tries to drag him away. The piano lid falls with a crash on PINKY's hands and he nurses his fingers as CHICOLINI leads him off.

They are seen in back view as they go towards the stairs.

Then in a medium close-up.

CHICOLINI: *You stay here, but keep quiet. Remember what she said. If we get caught, we're gonna get — uh — court-plastered.*

Back to the previous shot as CHICOLINI goes off up the stairs. Upstairs in his bedroom FIREFLY is lying in bed. The telephone rings and he wakes with a start and answers it.

MRS TEASDALE is in her bedroom, sitting on the bed.

MRS TEASDALE into the telephone: *Your Excellency, I'm worried. I can't sleep.*

In a long shot of FIREFLY's bedroom, CHICOLINI quietly opens the door in the foreground while FIREFLY replies into the phone:

FIREFLY: *What? You're worried? You can't sleep? That's fine. Now you woke me up. Now I can't sleep.*

We see MRS TEASDALE again.

MRS TEASDALE: *It's about those plans. I won't rest until they're back in your hands.*

At the bottom of the stairs, PINKY is listening in on the extension.

MRS TEASDALE continues.

MRS TEASDALE: *Won't you please come over and get them?*

Back to FIREFLY.

FIREFLY: *Oh, the plans? Okay. I'll be right over.*

A longer shot includes CHICOLINI, who comes into the room in the foreground as FIREFLY hangs up and gets out of bed. He goes into the bathroom, and CHICOLINI leaps across the

147

bed and locks him in.

We see CHICOLINI's hand locking the door. FIREFLY rattles the handle from inside.

CHICOLINI runs back across the room towards us as FIREFLY shouts from the bathroom.

FIREFLY off : *Let me out!*

In a reverse shot, CHICOLINI exits into the dressing room.

FIREFLY off : *Let me out.*

Down in the hall, PINKY hangs up the extension phone; he gets an idea, and camera pans as he starts up the staircase.

Upstairs, CHICOLINI comes back into FIREFLY's bedroom, dressing himself in FIREFLY's nightclothes. There is pounding from the bathroom off-screen.

FIREFLY off : *Let me out! Hey, let me out of here, or throw me a magazine.*

More pounding; CHICOLINI puts on a pair of glasses and paints himself a moustache.

FIREFLY off : *So that's your game, eh? I'll huff and I'll puff and I'll blow your door in.* He blows.

Camera pans with CHICOLINI as he goes to the door of the bedroom and exits.

In the corridor at the top of the stairs, CHICOLINI appears disguised as FIREFLY, and runs across to a door in the background.

MRS TEASDALE is pacing nervously to and fro in her bedroom. There is a knock at the door.

MRS TEASDALE : *Come in.*

CHICOLINI enters, disguised as FIREFLY, complete with a cigar. Shot of the two of them as CHICOLINI comes up to her and slaps his thigh.

MRS TEASDALE : *Oh, your Excellency! I'm so glad you've come.*

CHICOLINI removing his cigar : *I'm glad I come, too. You gotta da plans?*

He lopes across the room in front of her, imitating FIREFLY.

MRS TEASDALE : *Why, your Excellency! You sound so strange. Why are you talking like that?*

CHICOLINI : *Oh, well, you see, maybe some time maybe I go to Italy and I'm practising da language.*

In FIREFLY's bedroom, PINKY is also disguising himself as

148

Firefly. He paints on a moustache, then puts on some glasses and a nightcap. More pounding from the bathroom off-screen. Pinky puts a cigar in his mouth and admires the effect in a handmirror.

Firefly off : *I'll see my lawyer about this as soon as he graduates from law school.*

More pounding. Camera pans with Pinky as he goes to the door.

We return to Mrs Teasdale and Chicolini.

Mrs Teasdale : *Your dialect is perfect. I could listen to you all night.*

A closer shot of the two of them.

Chicolini : *'At'sa all right, but I can't stay here all night.* In a conspiratorial whisper : *Where's the plans?*

Mrs Teasdale : *They're in the safe downstairs. I'll write out the combination.*

Outside, Pinky crosses the corridor to Mrs Teasdale's door, skipping as he goes.

In the bedroom, Mrs Teasdale goes to look in her dressing table. The door opens off-screen; Chicolini looks off and dives under the bed . . .

As Pinky enters and slams the door. Camera tracks with him as he lopes across the room, cigar in mouth, imitating Firefly's walk.

In a medium shot, Mrs Teasdale turns to find Pinky behind her, ferreting about on the dressing table.

Mrs Teasdale : *Oh, there you are. Here's the combination. Is that clear?*

She gives him a piece of paper on which she has written the combination, and Pinky tucks it in the pocket of his nightshirt. At that moment Chicolini sticks his head out from under the bed behind them.

Close-up of Chicolini : he dodges back under the bed again.

Resume on Pinky and Mrs Teasdale.

Mrs Teasdale : *Is there anything else you want to know?*

Pinky takes the cigar from his mouth and grins. She looks at him curiously.

Mrs Teasdale : *What's the matter with you? Have you lost your voice?*

149

Pinky clutches his horn under his nightgown. It makes a loud burping noise and Mrs Teasdale starts back, somewhat embarrassed.

Mrs Teasdale : *Let me get you a glass of water, your* . . .

Cut to a medium shot.

Mrs Teasdale : . . . *Excellency.*

She bows low to him and goes to the back of the room. Pinky bows also and loses his nightcap, revealing his blond hair. He bends to pick it up, and comes nose to nose with Chicolini as he sticks his head out from under the bed again.

In a closer shot, they exchange glances, as Pinky replaces his night cap, looking alarmed.

Back to the scene : Mrs Teasdale turns holding a glass of water while Pinky makes for the door, and Chicolini disappears under the bed again.

Mrs Teasdale : *Your Excellency* . . .

We see them by the door as Mrs Teasdale approaches with the glass.

Mrs Teasdale : . . . *here's your water.*

Pinky exits through the door, head down, flapping his hand at her.

Mrs Teasdale : *What in the world's the matter with him?*

In a shot from the end of the bed, Mrs Teasdale starts taking off her dressing gown, while Chicolini crawls out from under the bed. She turns to find him behind her and hastily draws the dressing gown around her again.

Mrs Teasdale : *Oh!* Sternly : *Your Excellency, I thought you'd left.*

Chicolini : *Oh, no, I no leave.*

Mrs Teasdale : *But I saw you with my own eyes.*

Chicolini : *Well, who you gonna believe, me or your own eyes?*

Mrs Teasdale turning round and round : *Oh! Your Excellency, I'm sorry, but this excitement's too much for me. I feel faint. Ohh!*

She lies back on the bed, clutching at her forehead.

Chicolini : *Wait. I get you a glass of water.*

In Firefly's bedroom, there is more pounding at the bathroom door. Then Firefly finally breaks it open and comes out. He starts towards the bedroom door.

Out in the corridor, Firefly appears in the foreground, looks to and fro, and makes for Mrs Teasdale's bedroom in the background.

Mrs Teasdale is lying on her bed in a faint. There is a knock at the door and Chicolini dives under the bed. Camera pans to include the door as Firefly enters.

In a shot across the bed, Mrs Teasdale is seen stretched out in the foreground while Firefly comes forward, peering suspiciously round the room. He notices Mrs Teasdale, who waves an arm and says feebly :

Mrs Teasdale : *How about my glass of water?*

Firefly : *I give up. How about your glass of water?* He goes on peering to and fro.

Long shot of the stairs from the bottom : Pinky comes hurtling down clutching the piece of paper with the combination on it, skids on the marble in his bedsocks, back-pedals wildly and finally runs off in the foreground.

In the drawing room, Pinky is reflected in a large mirror in the background as he appears in front of camera and searches to and fro. He spots something on the right and we follow him as he goes up to a radio with a central dial which looks like a safe, standing on a table by the wall.

Shot of his hands holding the piece of paper with the safe combination written on it :

TO RIGHT — 5
THEN LEFT — 3
THEN RIGHT   4

Resume on Pinky as he turns the dial, following the instructions. Suddenly, loud brass band music starts blaring from the radio. Pinky clutches at his ears, then flaps his hands helplessly at the machine.

In Mrs Teasdale's bedroom, she and Firefly stand at the door, listening to the noise from down below.

Back in the drawing room, the radio continues blaring as Pinky frantically turns the dial. It comes off in his hand. He throws it on the floor, then grabs a cushion and puts it on top of the radio, trying to muffle the sound; it has no effect, and he tries a curtain hanging beside him, then grabs a soda siphon and sprays it all over the radio. The music keeps on

151

blaring. Finally he picks up the radio and runs off.

Pinky runs across the drawing room with the radio, throws it into a closet and slams the door on it. It lands with a crash inside, but the music keeps on playing.

Up in the bedroom, Firefly is listening at the half-open door. He shuts it and turns to Mrs Teasdale.

Mrs Teasdale : *What's that?*

Firefly : *Sounds to me like mice.*

Mrs Teasdale : *Mice? Mice don't play music.*

Firefly : *No? How about the old maestro?*

Mrs Teasdale : *Oh!*

Resume on Pinky in the drawing room. He clutches at his ears, then opens the closet, picks up the blaring radio and brings it out again.

In a closer shot, he throws the radio on the floor with a crash. Still it plays. He stands flapping his hands in despair, then picks up a pedestal ashtray and starts smashing the thing up. More music. He gathers up the bits and runs off.

We move to the window. Pinky runs up and throws the radio

152

outside. He shuts the window and the music finally stops.

Up in the bedroom, Mrs Teasdale is sitting on the bed, while Firefly stands beside her talking into the phone.

Firefly : *Get me headquarters; not hindquarters — headquarters.*

Seen in close-up, Chicolini sticks his head out from under the bed.

Firefly off : *Hello.*

Resume on him and Mrs Teasdale.

Firefly : *Rush the guards right over to Mrs Teasdale's and have 'em surround the house.*

Down in the drawing room, Pinky turns away from the window and sees . . .

Firefly coming down the stairs.

Pinky looks panic-stricken and runs off.

He rushes across the drawing room and crashes straight into large mirror seen previously. It shatters on the floor.

Firefly, at the bottom of the stairs, hears the noise and lopes off towards the drawing room.

Camera pans with him as he runs across to the gap left by the smashed mirror (the alcove beyond is furnished in a mirror image of the drawing room). As he searches to and fro, Pinky peeps round the corner. They start simultaneously across the gap, but half way across Firefly notices Pinky, and they stop.

Shot of the two of them as they stare at one another. Firefly leans forward suspiciously; Pinky mirrors his actions.

Shot of the scene. Firefly walks away from the 'mirror' pondering; Pinky does likewise. Firefly turns suddenly, trying to catch him out; bends down and wiggles his behind; comes up to the mirror again. Pinky mirrors his every move.

Camera pans as they walk to the edge of the alcove. Firefly nods: 'You can't fool me'. Pinky does likewise, and disappears round the corner. Firefly has an idea; he peers forward round the edge of the alcove, and meets Pinky doing the same.

Close-up of Firefly. He has another idea.

He gets down on all fours and peers round the corner again — and meets Pinky doing the same. He gets up again.

Firefly ponders. He has a better idea.

153

He trots across the gap, high-stepping; so does PINKY. He
hops back sideways facing the 'mirror'; so does PINKY. They
skip across, jigging one leg up and down.

In a longer shot, FIREFLY walks slowly to the centre and does
a wild charleston, facing the mirror; PINKY does likewise,
grinning. FIREFLY spins round; PINKY doesn't, but strikes the
right pose when FIREFLY ends up facing him again. FIREFLY
moves to the edge of the alcove, fluttering his hands like part
of a negro hallelujah chorus; PINKY disappears round the
corner doing the same. FIREFLY has another idea and goes off.
Back to the previous shot as FIREFLY enters slowly with a
panama hat behind his back; PINKY does likewise, but we see
that he has his black top hat. Convinced that he's caught
him out this time, FIREFLY laughs and steps up to the
'mirror'; so does PINKY. They circle round through the
'mirror', reversing their positions. FIREFLY spots the black
hat and heaves with silent laughter — now he's got him —
and PINKY does the same. They circle back through the
'mirror', and suddenly FIREFLY puts on his hat.

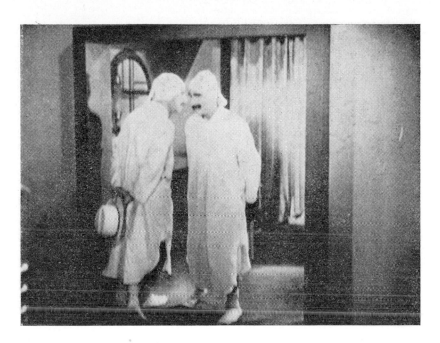

Seen in a closer shot, Pinky does likewise — producing a
panama hat he has been hiding. Firefly points — 'Haha, I
caught you'; Pinky mirrors him — 'Haha *I* caught *you*'.
Pinky is so pleased with himself that he points out of turn,
then pulls a face as he realizes.

Back to the scene as they both take off their hats and bow.
Pinky drops his and Firefly hands it back to him. Pinky grins
thank you. Firefly slowly puts his hat on and takes it off
again; Pinky does likewise, but getting more and more out
of phase.

A closer shot as Firefly, mirrored by Pinky, turns away and
ponders. At that moment, Chicolini enters on Pinky's side of
the 'mirror'. Pinky gazes in horror at his night-shirted figure
and hurriedly pushes him out of sight. He just recovers his
pose as Firefly turns towards him again. Chicolini wanders
on again and Pinky runs off, while Firefly grabs Chicolini
by the tail of his nightshirt and holds him fast.

The scene dissolves to a newspaper headline :

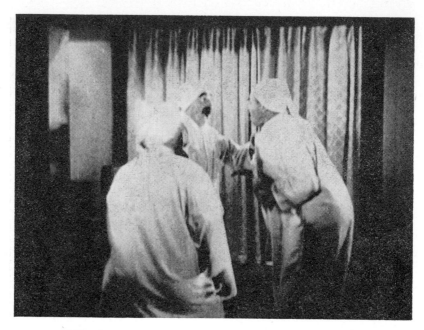

CHICOLINI UNDER ARREST; FACES COURT-MARTIAL FOR TREASON

SPY TRAPPED ATTEMPTING TO STEAL WAR PLANS AT GLORIA TEASDALE HOME.

Firefly to prosecute: quick conviction is promised.

Dissolve again to the Freedonian Council Chamber, seen from a very high angle, filled with ministers, generals, trumpeters and guards, and the Freedonian people in rustic dress. A LACKEY steps forward and announces:

LACKEY : *His Excellency, Rufus T. Firefly.*

Music; the people sing.

PEOPLE singing : *Hail, hail Freedonia,*
         Land of . . .

A closer shot looking down on the scene as FIREFLY enters.

PEOPLE singing : *. . . the brave and free.*

Camera pans with FIREFLY as he steps up to his desk at the end of the council table. BOB and the ministers are waiting for him.

We now see BOB in the foreground. The ministers sit down,

while FIREFLY opens his brief case and takes out his lunch.

FIREFLY: *Lieutenant . . .* BOB springs to his feet . . . *why weren't the original indictment papers placed in my portfolio?*

He pours himself a glass of milk.

BOB: *Why . . . er . . . I didn't think those papers were important at this time, your Excellency.*

Shot of the two of them, with a GENERAL sitting beside them.

FIREFLY: *You didn't think they were important? You realize I had my dessert wrapped in those papers?* He hands the empty milk bottle to the GENERAL. *Here, take this bottle back and get two cents for it.*

Cut to show CHICOLINI in the dock. He gets up with a cheery wave, and shouts across to FIREFLY.

CHICOLINI: *Hello, boss!*

We see FIREFLY seated at the bench, flanked by the JUDGE, the GENERAL and the ministers. CHICOLINI is in the dock in the foreground.

FIREFLY: *Chicolini, I'll bet you eight to one we find you guilty.*

CHICOLINI: *'At'sa no good. 1 can get ten to one at the barber shop.*

The PROSECUTOR enters from the left.

PROSECUTOR: *Chicolini, you are charged with high treason, and if found guilty, you'll be shot.*

He is seen in back view, standing over CHICOLINI.

CHICOLINI: *I object.*

PROSECUTOR: *Huh! You object! On what grounds?*

CHICOLINI: *I couldn't think of anything else to say.*

FIREFLY is seen from a low angle with the GENERAL beside him. He bangs the gavel on the table.

FIREFLY: *Objection sustained.*

Resume on CHICOLINI and the PROSECUTOR.

PROSECUTOR turning to FIREFLY: *Your Excellency! You* sustain *the objection?*

Back to FIREFLY and the GENERAL.

FIREFLY: *Sure. I couldn't think of anything else to say, either. Why don't you object?*

Shot of the whole bench, with the PROSECUTOR and CHICOLINI in the foreground.

PROSECUTOR: *Chicolini, when were you born?*

Resume on just the two of them.

157

CHICOLINI : *I don't remember. I was just a little baby.*

PROSECUTOR : *Isn't it true you tried to sell Freedonia's secret war code and plans?*

CHICOLINI : *Sure. I sold a code and two pair of plans.* He laughs and slaps the edge of the desk.

Back to the scene.

CHICOLINI to FIREFLY : *'At's some joke, eh, boss?*

FIREFLY : *Now I'll bet you twenty to one we find you guilty!*

Shot of the JUDGE.

JUDGE : *Chicolini, have you anyone here to defend you?*

Back to CHICOLINI and the PROSECUTOR.

CHICOLINI : *It'sa no use. I even offered to pay as high as eighteen dollars, but I no coulda get someone to defend me.*

Resume on the bench.

FIREFLY : *My friends, this man's case moves me deeply.*

He climbs over the desk and jumps to the floor, then we cut back to CHICOLINI, head bowed.

FIREFLY off : *Look at Chicolini!*

Resume on the scene.

FIREFLY dramatically : *He sits there alone, an abject figure.*

CHICOLINI : *I abject!*

FIREFLY declaiming : *I say look at Chicolini. He sits there alone, a pitiable object* . . . In an aside to CHICOLINI : *Let's see you get out of that one!* . . . *Surrounded by a* . . .

Shot of the crowd of Freedonians watching in the gallery.

FIREFLY off : . . . *sea of unfriendly* . . .

Then another part of the crowd.

FIREFLY off : . . . *faces.*

We now see FIREFLY standing over CHICOLINI, with the people above him in the background.

FIREFLY : *Chicolini, give me a number from one to ten.*

CHICOLINI : *Eleven.*

FIREFLY : *Right.*

CHICOLINI : *Now, I ask you one. What is it has a trunk, but no key, weighs two thousand pounds and lives in a circus?*

Cut to include the PROSECUTOR in the foreground.

PROSECUTOR : *That's irrelevant.*

CHICOLINI : *A relephant! Hey, that's the answer. There's a whole lotta relephants in a circus.*

Shot of the JUDGE.

JUDGE : *That sort of testimony we can eliminate.*

Resume on FIREFLY and CHICOLINI.

CHICOLINI : *'At'sa fine. I'll take some.*

The JUDGE again.

JUDGE : *You'll take what?*

Back to FIREFLY and CHICOLINI.

CHICOLINI : *Eliminate. A nice cold glass eliminate.* To FIREFLY : *Hey, boss, I'm goin' good, eh?* He laughs. *Yeah.*

FIREFLY addressing the bench : *Gentlemen, Chicolini here may talk like an idiot, and look like an idiot, but don't let that fool you. He really is an idiot. I implore you, send him back to his father and brothers who are waiting for him with open arms in the penitentiary. I suggest that we give him ten years in Leavenworth, or eleven years in Twelveworth.*

CHICOLINI : *I tell you what I'll do. I'll take five and ten in Woolworth.*

FIREFLY : *I wanted to get a writ of habeas corpus, but I should have gotten a writ of you instead.*

A longer shot includes the PROSECUTOR, the JUDGE and the people in the background.

PROSECUTOR : *I object!*

FIREFLY : *Even I object.*

CHICOLINI : *Then I object too.*

Shot of the JUDGE.

JUDGE : *You're on trial. You can't object.*

Resume on the scene as a military courier enters in the background.

COURIER : *Your Excellency! General Cooper says that the Sylvanian troops are about to land on Freedonia's soil. This means war!*

He goes out again as the MINISTER OF FINANCE leaps up in the foreground.

MINISTER OF FINANCE : *Something must be done! War would mean a prohibitive increase in our taxes.*

Shot of CHICOLINI, FIREFLY and the MINISTER OF FINANCE.

CHICOLINI : *Hey, I got an uncle lives in Taxes.*

MINISTER OF FINANCE : *No. I'm talking about taxes — money — dollars.*

CHICOLINI : *Dollas! That's where my uncle lives. Dollas, Taxes.*

159

He laughs and shakes hands with FIREFLY.

MINISTER OF FINANCE : *Aww!*

Back to the scene again as the PROSECUTOR sits CHICOLINI down in the dock while FIREFLY shakes hands with the MINISTER OF FINANCE. The trumpeters enter in the background and blow a fanfare.

FIREFLY : *More bad news!*

Some guards come in and flank the entrance with crossed swords as MRS TEASDALE hurries in after them.

FIREFLY : *Didn't I tell you?*

MRS TEASDALE : *Your Excellency!*

Shot of the two of them.

FIREFLY : *What's on your mind, babe?*

MRS TEASDALE clasping his arm : *On behalf of the women of Freedonia, I have taken it upon myself to make one final effort to prevent war.*

The guards march out in the background.

FIREFLY : *No kidding!*

MRS TEASDALE : *I've talked to Ambassador Trentino and he says Sylvania doesn't want war either.*

FIREFLY : *Eether.*

MRS TEASDALE : *Doesn't want war eether.*

FIREFLY : *Either.*

MRS TEASDALE sighs.

FIREFLY : *Skip it.*

MRS TEASDALE : *I've taken the liberty of asking the Ambassador to come over here because we both felt that a friendly conference would settle everything peacefully. He'll be here any moment.*

Music over another shot of the two of them.

FIREFLY patting her hand : *Mrs. Teasdale, you did a noble deed!* Camera pans as he walks across in front of her. *I'd be unworthy of the high trust that's been placed in me if I didn't do everything within my power to keep our beloved Freedonia at peace with the world. I'll be only too happy to meet Ambassador Trentino and offer him, on behalf of my country, the right hand of good fellowship.* Jovially : *And I feel sure that he will accept this gesture in the spirit in which it is offered . . . But suppose he doesn't? A fine thing that'll be! I hold out my hand and he refuses to accept it! That'll add a lot to my prestige, won't it.* He starts shouting indignantly.

160

Me, the head of a country, snubbed by a foreign ambassador! Who does he think he is that he can come here and make a sap out of me in front of all my people? Think of it!

Shot of the scene. Camera pans as he moves back across her again. The music continues.

FIREFLY working himself up: *I hold out my hand and that hyena refuses to accept it! Why, the cheap, four-flushing swine! He'll never get away with it, I tell you!*

MRS TEASDALE: *Oh!*

FIREFLY: *He'll never get away with it.*

At that moment, TRENTINO enters with a retinue of Sylvanian officers.

MRS TEASDALE: *Oh please!*

FIREFLY rounds on TRENTINO before he can get a word out.

FIREFLY: *So! You refuse to shake hands with me, eh?*

He slaps TRENTINO with his gloves. The music stops. MRS TEASDALE wails:

MRS TEASDALE: *Ohhh!*

They are all seen from a low angle. TRENTINO is furious.

TRENTINO waving his forefinger: *Mrs Teasdale, this is the last straw! There's no turning back now. This means war!*

He goes out with the Sylvanian officers, followed by MRS TEASDALE.

FIREFLY: *Then it's war!*

Back to the scene. We follow FIREFLY as he strides to the head of the council table. The trumpeters raise their instruments.

FIREFLY: *Then it's war!*

Fanfare.

FIREFLY: *Then it's war!*

Fanfare.

FIREFLY: *Gather the forces!*

Fanfare.

FIREFLY: *Harness the horses!*

Fanfare.

FIREFLY: *Then it's war!*

Music, as the JUDGE, in close-up, rises and salutes.

The GENERAL does the same.

Then a minister.

And another minister, who sings.

MINISTER singing : *Freedonia's going to war!*
Back to the GENERAL.
GENERAL singing : *Each native son will grab a gun.*
Shot of a stenographer.
STENOGRAPHER singing : *And run away to war!*
Camera shows a row of generals and ministers with the Freedonian people in the background.
ALL singing : *At last we're going to . . .*
Shot of FIREFLY, BOB and the ministers at the bench.
ALL singing : *Feet will beat along the street to . . . war!*
Resume on the scene as BOB exits. The music continues.
ALL singing : *We're going to war!*
CHICOLINI appears from under the council table.
CHICOLINI singing : *We're going to war!*
GUARDS singing : *We're going to war!*
FIREFLY crawls under the table, then we cut to show CHICOLINI appearing over the top of the table with FIREFLY on all fours beneath.
CHICOLINI : *We're going to war!*
Sound of drums, as we see the entrance to the council chamber. Camera pans as PINKY marches in at the head of a group of guards, twirling a drum-major's baton.
In a closer shot, PINKY halts and marks time, wielding the baton, as the guards form up in a row behind him. He throws the baton high in the air and it brings a large crystal chandelier crashing down on his head. He extricates himself from the chandelier and goes off while BOB, FIREFLY and CHICOLINI enter behind the row of guards.
We hear xylophone music as CHICOLINI, BOB and FIREFLY play on the guards' helmets with sticks.
The guards mark time to the music as a longer shot includes PINKY, who has joined in at the end of the row, and the ministers watching in the foreground.
Seen in a closer shot again, the guards turn and start marching out. PINKY produces his scissors and starts snipping at the plumes on their helmets.
PINKY snips off the plumes as the guards march past in front of him.
As the guards march out, seen from below, PINKY grabs his

drum-major's baton and hits the last one over the head with it. We look down on the whole scene. As the guards file out in the centre, everyone gets up and starts surging to and fro.

ALL singing : *To war, to war, to war we're gonna go!*
FIREFLY, BOB, CHICOLINI and PINKY sing in a row, fluttering their hands like a negro chorus.

THE FOUR singing: *Oh, hi-de, hi-de, hi-de, hi-de, hi-de, hi-de-ho.* Shot of the scene as everyone sings, shaking their fists in emphasis.

ALL singing : *To war, to war, to war we're gonna go.*
The four sing again on their knees, fluttering their hands.

THE FOUR singing: *Oh, hi-de, hi-de, hi-de, hi-de, hi-de, hi-de-ho.* Back to the scene as they stop and everyone else takes up the refrain, fluttering their hands.

ALL singing : *Oh, hi-de, hi-de, hi-de, hi-de, hi-de, hi-de-ho.*
The four kick up their legs as they sing.

THE FOUR singing: *Oh, hi-de, hi-de, hi-de, hi-de, hi-de, hi-de-ho.* We look down on the scene as they stop and everyone else kicks up their legs.

ALL singing: *Oh, hi-de, hi-de, hi-de, hi-de, hi-de, hi-de-ho.*

163

Firefly, Bob, Chicolini and Pinky sing, hauling on an imaginary rope.

The Four : *Oh-ho, oh-ho, oh-ho, oh-ho, oh-ho.*

Resume on the scene. They stop and everyone else starts rope-hauling.

All singing : *Oh-ho, oh-ho, oh-ho, oh-ho, oh-ho, hoooooooo . . .*

Back to the group, with the people behind.

All singing : *Hoooooooo.*

Camera tracks out as the four advance towards us with watermelon grins, swaying from side to side.

The Four singing : *They got guns,*
　　　　　　　We got guns,
　　　　　　　All God's chillun got guns.

They turn away from camera, which pans to show the people swinging their arms.

All singing : *We gonna walk all o'er the battlefield*
　　　　　　'Cause all God's chillun got guns.

Pan back to the group, sitting up on the judges' bench, strumming banjos, then cut to a closer shot of them.

The Four singing : *Oh, Freedonia,*
　　　　　　　Oh donya cry for me,
　　　　　　　We're comin' round the mountain
　　　　　　　With a banjo on my knee.

They jump down from the bench and we cut back to the scene as they advance towards camera, playing their banjos.

All singing : *Oh, Freedonia,*
　　　　　　Oh, donya cry for me.

The Four singing : *We're comin' round the mountain . . .*

They kneel with their banjos, seen in a medium close-up.

The Four singing : *With a banjo on my . . .*

Cut to include the people around them as they get up and start a country-style dance. Music.

We look down on the scene as everyone gets up and dances round, shouting to the music.

The four are seen dancing amidst the people, then we cut in to Firefly, Bob and Chicolini. The trumpets sound and everyone freezes, listening.

All singing, hands to ears : *To war, to war, to war we're gonna go.*

Seen in a medium shot, everyone advances towards camera,

with Firefly, Bob and Chicolini in the centre.

All singing : *To war, to war, to war . . .*

A violin is heard off-screen, and we cut to show Pinky playing it, surrounded by the people.

A closer shot of Pinky with the people dancing behind him. He plays the violin above his head, behind his back, then finds he's lost the bow. He turns round — the bow is sticking out of the back of his trousers.

Resume on Chicolini, Bob and Firefly with the people behind. There is another fanfare and they all hearken.

All singing : *To war, to war,*
  We soon will say goodbye.

Cut in on the three of them.

Bob singing tearfully : *Oh, how we'd cry for Firefly,*
  If Firefly should die.

We look down on the whole scene.

All singing : *A mighty man is he.*

The people of Freedonia, in a medium shot, start surging down from the gallery.

All singing : *A man of brawn who'll carry on*
  Till dawn of . . .

Cut in on them jumping over the benches.

All singing : *. . . victory.*
  With him to lead the way . . .

Seen in reverse angle they surge towards the council table where everyone has gathered, and turn to face camera.

All singing : *Our spirits will not lag,*
  Until the judgement day.

We look down on the council table. Everyone throws up their hands and sings.

All singing : *We'll rally round the flag, the flag, the flag!*

Dissolve to the Freedonian flag, which is drawn aside revealing Firefly, Chicolini, Pinky and Bob, posing as statues in 18th century soldier's costumes. Pinky is mounted on a horse. There is a roll of drums.

Shot of the group as Firefly looks off, sabre in hand.

Firefly : *The enemy is coming. There'll be two lamps in the steeple if they're coming by land, and one if they're coming by sea.* He exits.

165

He reappears at a casement window and opens it. It is night. One, two, then three lamps appear at the top of a church tower in the distance.

FIREFLY turning: *They've double-crossed me! They're coming by land and sea.* He starts out.

Resume on CHICOLINI, PINKY and BOB in the same pose as before. FIREFLY enters and shouts to PINKY, waving his sabre.

FIREFLY: *Ride through every village and town,*
Wake every citizen up hill and down.

FIREFLY is seen from a low angle.

FIREFLY: *Tell 'em the enemy comes from afar,*
He dances a jig.
With a hey nonny-nonny and a ha-cha-cha.

Resume on the group as BOB and CHICOLINI exit to the left.

FIREFLY waving his sabre: *Be off, my lad.*

PINKY rides his horse down from the plinth and off in the foreground. Dramatic music begins.

The scene dissolves to the streets of Freedonia at night. Camera tracks with PINKY in close-up as he gallops along, blowing a bugle. Sound of hoofbeats as the music continues.

Dissolve to a shot of a darkened street. People run out of the houses as PINKY gallops towards us, blowing his bugle.

Resume on the tracking shot; PINKY blows his bugle.

He passes down another street and gallops off. People run out in their nightshirts, one carrying a lantern.

Seen from a high angle, PINKY slows to a halt. He looks off and grins as he sees . . .

A girl undressing through a window.

PINKY dismounts and goes off in the foreground, grinning, while the music changes to ' Ain't she sweet?'

Inside the house, the GIRL comes into the bathroom in her underclothes and turns on the bath tap.

While PINKY strides into the bedroom in his Paul Revere outfit, his bugle slung round his neck. Camera pans with him to the bathroom door.

Resume on the bathroom. PINKY opens the door and looks in, sees the GIRL bent over the bath and goes out again.

Outside the house, we follow PINKY as he comes down the

steps to his horse, which is standing in the foreground. He takes a nosebag from the saddle and puts it on the horse.

Cut to show the horse tossing its head, eating, as PINKY goes up the steps into the house again in the background.

We return to the bedroom, where the GIRL is now in a dressing gown. She looks up in surprise as PINKY leaps in through the door and lands with a crash.

GIRL : *Oh!*

Camera pans as he advances on her lustfully and she backs away, gasping.

Outside, the LEMONADE VENDOR is seen from above, coming up the steps.

In the bedroom, PINKY is lolling on the bed while the GIRL looks out of the window. She hurries across to him and he gets up.

GIRL : *My husband! Quick!* She pushes him towards the bathroom. *Hide in there!*

In a closer shot, he tries to pull her into the bathroom with him. There is a violent struggle.

GIRL : *Oh, don't!*

She finally breaks free; PINKY exits into the bathroom and the door slams.

Resume on the scene in the bedroom as the VENDOR strides in through the door. The GIRL goes up to him hurriedly from beside the bed and thrusts a gun into his hands.

GIRL : *Freedonia's going to war!*

He hands it back, ignoring her, and says :

VENDOR : *I'm goin' to take a bath!*

GIRL : *Oh!*

She watches desperately, holding the gun, as camera follows the VENDOR to the bathroom door. He goes in.

Dissolve to show the VENDOR in the bathroom, a little later, sitting in the bathtub. He leans back and PINKY's hooter sounds.

The VENDOR, in close-up, looks up in surprise. He looks round, then underneath him.

Back to the scene as he sits down in the bath again. The horn sounds from underneath him.

The VENDOR looks round again, bewildered.

He sits back in the bath again. The horn sounds long and loud from underneath.

The VENDOR starts, in close-up, as PINKY's bugle sounds a loud fanfare . . .

And PINKY rises from the tub in front of the VENDOR, sopping wet and blowing his bugle.

VENDOR: *Oh!*

PINKY drops the bugle and runs for the door, while the VENDOR buries his face in his hands.

Dissolve to another street as PINKY appears on his horse and stops beneath a window with a girl looking out. Romantic music.

Seen from below, the girl waves invitingly and blows a kiss. Camera tilts down onto PINKY as he rides through the doorway and into the house.

Dissolve to the bedroom in the house: we see PINKY's boots lying under the bed, then camera pans to show the girl's slippers next to them, and finally four horse shoes lying on the floor. A clock strikes three.

Shot of the bedroom. PINKY and the horse are sharing a double bed in the foreground, while the girl is in a single bed beyond. They are all asleep. Fade out.

The scene changes to FIREFLY's war headquarters. Bombs and shells are heard exploding intermittently off-screen. We follow FIREFLY as he paces to and fro, accompanied by his military staff. He consults a map, then crosses to the wireless set. Camera tracks in as he addresses the operator.

FIREFLY: *Clear all the wires.*

The wireless crackles, and FIREFLY dictates a message.

FIREFLY: *The enemy has captured hills 27 and 28, throwing thirteen hill-billies out of work. Last night two snipers crept into our machine gun nest and laid an egg. Send reinforcements immediately. Send that off collect.*

He paces across the room again and a GENERAL enters in the background.

Cut to the two of them; as they talk, the wireless crackles and the shells explode in the distance.

GENERAL: *Your Excellency, our men are being badly beaten in*

168

open warfare. I suggest we dig trenches.
FIREFLY: *Dig trenches? With our men being killed off like flies? There isn't time to dig trenches. We'll have to buy 'em ready made. Here, run out and get some trenches.* He hands him a note.
GENERAL saluting: *Yes sir.* He starts out.
FIREFLY: *Wait a minute.*

The GENERAL pauses. FIREFLY holds a hand up at chin-level.
FIREFLY: *Get 'em this high and our soldiers won't need any pants.*
GENERAL saluting: *Yes, sir.* He starts out again.
FIREFLY: *Wait a minute.*

The GENERAL pauses. FIREFLY holds a hand above his head.
FIREFLY: *Get 'em this high and we won't need any soldiers.*
GENERAL: *Yes, sir.* He goes out.

In the Sylvanian headquarters, TRENTINO is seated at a table with CHICOLINI and an officer standing on either side. CHICOLINI is wearing Freedonian uniform. The sound of shells continues.
TRENTINO: *Chicolini, your partner's deserted us, but I'm still counting on you. There's a machine-gun nest near Hill 28. I want it cleaned out.*
CHICOLINI: *All right, I'll tell the janitor.*

Back in the Freedonian headquarters, FIREFLY is pacing up and down — now wearing a Unionist uniform. BOB hurries in in the background.
BOB: *A message from the front, sir.* He hands him an envelope.
There are distant explosions as we cut to a shot of the two of them.
FIREFLY: *I'm sick of messages from the front. Don't we ever get any messages from the side?* He takes the envelope and opens it, holding it so that BOB can't see. *What is it?*
BOB: *General Smith reports a gas attack. He wants to know what to do.*
FIREFLY: *Tell him to take a teaspoonful of bicarbonate in a half a glass of water.*
BOB saluting: *Yes, sir.*

He exits. FIREFLY hears a crackle from the wireless and looks off.
Shot of FIREFLY and his officers. Camera follows him to the wireless post.

169

FIREFLY : *Any answer to that message?*

OPERATOR : *No, sir.*

FIREFLY : *Well, in that case don't send it.*

> He moves away and looks out of the window in the background, followed by the officers. There is the whine of a shell.
> Seen in a long shot. FIREFLY and the officers duck as a shell flies through the window . . .
> Crashes through a wall on the other side of the room and explodes outside.
> FIREFLY and his staff rush across the room.
> They appear in the foreground and go up to the large gap in the wall made by the shell. FIREFLY bends down amongst the rubble.
> Medium shot of FIREFLY and the officers. He picks up a straw boater with its crown flapping.

FIREFLY : *Gentlemen, this is the last straw. Where's my Stradivarius?*

A GENERAL : *Here, sir.* He hands him a violin case.

> Camera pans with FIREFLY as he puts the case on a table and takes out a machine gun.

FIREFLY : *I'll show 'em they can't fiddle around with old Firefly.*

> We now see him through the gap in the wall. The officers scatter in the background as FIREFLY looses off a burst with the machine gun.

FIREFLY : *Look at 'em run. Now they know they've been in a war.*

> BOB comes up behind him.

BOB saluting : *Your Excellency!*

> The two of them are seen facing camera. FIREFLY swings the gun to and fro, imitating the noise of it firing and laughing gleefully.

FIREFLY : *They're fleeing like rats.*

BOB : *But sir, I've got to tell you . . .*

> We see them from the side.

FIREFLY : *Remind me to give myself the Firefly medal for this.*

> He fires another burst.

BOB : *But your Excellency, you're shooting your own men.*

> FIREFLY stops firing and turns to him.

FIREFLY : *What?*

BOB : *You're shooting your own men.*

171

172

FIREFLY puts down the gun and produces some notes from his pocket.

FIREFLY : *Here's five dollars. Keep it under your hat. Never mind. I'll keep it under my hat.*

He holds out his hat. BOB puts in the money and exits.

Two officers stand talking as the explosions continue in the distance.

FIRST OFFICER : *Now we've got to have more men or we're lost.*

SECOND OFFICER : *Don't be alarmed. I've got a man combing the countryside for volunteers.*

Shot of a battlefield. There are loud explosions; tanks rumble past amid smoke. In the foreground, PINKY stands with his back to us, wearing a cocked hat and a sandwich board, which reads : JOIN THE ARMY AND SEE THE NAVY. A shell bursts in front of him and smoke fills the screen.

Resume on the headquarters, where we follow FIREFLY as he crosses the room, now wearing a Confederate uniform. The GENERAL seen earlier enters in the background and camera tracks in on him and FIREFLY.

GENERAL : *Your Excellency, the army's morale is crumbling. The men are breaking ranks.*

FIREFLY : *Where's the Secretary of War?*

GENERAL : *That's it! Where is the Secretary of War? The soldiers are waiting for his orders.*

A sentry appears in the background and announces :

SENTRY : *His Excellency, the Secretary of War!*

CHICOLINI enters and clocks in at the time clock by the door. He comes up to FIREFLY and the GENERAL and salutes.

Shot of the three of them. The explosions continue off. FIREFLY takes off his hat and bows sarcastically.

FIREFLY : *Awfully decent of you to drop in today. Do you realize our army's facing disastrous defeat? What do you intend to do about it?*

CHICOLINI : *I've done it already.*

FIREFLY : *You've done what?*

CHICOLINI : *I've changed to the other side.*

Cut and pan with FIREFLY and CHICOLINI as they walk across the room.

FIREFLY : *So you're on the other side, eh? Well, what are you doing*

173

over here?

CHICOLINI : *Well, the food is better over there.*

They hear the whine of a shell and we cut to a long shot. FIREFLY, CHICOLINI and the GENERAL all duck as shell flies in through the window and across the room.

Seen in a closer shot, they turn to look as the shell crashes through the wall off-screen and explodes.

FIREFLY appears at the window the shell entered by and pulls down the blind. Then he goes off again . . .

And comes back to CHICOLINI and the GENERAL.

FIREFLY : *Chicolini, I need you badly right now. What'll you take to come back and work for me again?*

CHICOLINI : *I'll take a vacation.*

FIREFLY : *Good! You're hired. Now, go out in that battlefield and lead those men to victory. Go on, they're waiting for you.*

As he speaks, he takes a canvas bag down from the wall and hangs it round CHICOLINI's neck. Camera pans as he pushes CHICOLINI to the door. CHICOLINI looks out and sees . . .

A murky battlefield with tanks rumbling past amid loud explosions.

Resume on FIREFLY, CHICOLINI and the GENERAL. CHICOLINI turns away from the door and says :

CHICOLINI : *I wouldn't go out there unless I was in one of those big iron things go up and down like this. What do you call those things?*

FIREFLY : *Tanks.*

CHICOLINI : *You're welcome.* He goes out of the door.

The headquarters is seen from a distance as a shell hits it. There is a flash and a loud explosion.

We see MRS TEASDALE at the telephone.

MRS TEASDALE : *Your Excellency, you must come over here at once. There is danger over here.*

In the headquarters, FIREFLY is now wearing a scout uniform. He replies on the telephone :

FIREFLY : *Why not come over here? There's no danger here.*

Outside the headquarters, a line of Sylvanian soldiers appear over a bank of sandbags, firing.

At a wooden barricade in front of the headquarters, PINKY is reloading his gun.

A soldier fires a shot from the line of sandbags . . .
And PINKY's cocked hat spins round once.
A soldier fires a burst with a machine gun . . .
And PINKY's hat whirls round like a windmill. He clutches at it nervously.
We see MRS TEASDALE again, sitting at a table in what appears to be a farmhouse kitchen. FIREFLY, CHICOLINI and BOB enter in the background. FIREFLY is now wearing a bearskin on his head.
In a medium shot of the group, she turns to face them; they put their fingers to their lips.
FIREFLY : *Sssh!*
MRS TEASDALE springs joyfully to her feet.
MRS TEASDALE : *Rufus!*
Cut to a longer shot as she tries to throw herself into his arms, but FIREFLY dodges. He and the other two make for the table and descend on a bowl of fruit like starving men.
Another shot of Sylvanian soldiers firing over a line of sandbags.
Resume on MRS TEASDALE, FIREFLY and CHICOLINI crouching by the window. FIREFLY restrains CHICOLINI, who is about to look out.
FIREFLY : *Wait a minute. I want to find out something.*
He takes a plate from a dresser and holds it up above the window sill. Nothing happens.
FIREFLY : *Just as I thought. The coast is clear.*
He stands up and his bearskin is immediately shot off his head. He falls to the floor.
MRS TEASDALE : *Rufus!*
FIREFLY : *Chicolini, to your post!*
CHICOLINI climbs on a box with his gun and takes aim through the window.
FIREFLY : *Remember you're fighting for this woman's honour —
which is probably more than she ever did.*
He gets up and takes aim also; at that moment BOB runs in.
BOB loudly : *Your Excellency!*
FIREFLY starts at the sound and drops his gun out of the window.
FIREFLY : *There goes my gun.* To MRS TEASDALE : *Run out and*

175

get that like a good girl.

MRS TEASDALE : *Oh, I'm afraid.*

BOB : *We can't last much longer. Our ammunition supplies are very low.*

FIREFLY : *Man the boats, Lieutenant. I'll get help.*

We see the house from a distance as a shell hits it. There is a flash and a loud explosion.

Inside the house, the ceiling starts to fall in, and a great beam nearly kills FIREFLY in the foreground. Camera pans as he runs to the wireless set by the wall.

Shot of him holding the microphone.

FIREFLY : *Calling all nations! Calling all nations! This is Rufus T....*

A shower of plaster and rubble falls on his head; he puts on a tin helmet and then continues.

FIREFLY : *This is Rufus T. Firefly, coming to you through the courtesy of the enemy.*

Cut to show PINKY coming in through the door.

FIREFLY off : *We're in a mess, folks, we're in a mess!*

176

Resume on FIREFLY at the microphone.

FIREFLY: *Rush to Freedonia. Three men and one woman are trapped in a building. Send help at once. If you can't send help, send two more women.*

At the door, PINKY holds up three fingers.

And FIREFLY adds:

FIREFLY: *Make it three more women.*

We see the house from a distance as another shell hits it and there is a loud explosion.

Resume on the four men in the ruined kitchen. FIREFLY is now wearing a raccoon hat.

BOB: *Your Excellency, we can't hold out much longer. We must have help.*

PINKY grins and slaps himself on the chest, then exits.

Seen from outside, PINKY opens the door, hangs up a sign which says HELP WANTED, and goes back into the house.

Inside, FIREFLY, BOB and CHICOLINI walk towards camera, FIREFLY first.

FIREFLY: *One of us has to break through the lines and get a*

177

word to General Cooper and his men.

We hear the whine of a shell off-screen.

FIREFLY : *Which one . . .*

There is a loud explosion as PINKY enters. They all look round.

FIREFLY : *Quiet back there! Which one of us . . .*

Cut to a closer shot.

FIREFLY : *. . . is going to have the rare privilege of sacrificing his life for his country?*

BOB : *We'll draw lots . . .*

CHICOLINI : *Wait, I got it!* He starts counting round the four of them. *Rrrrrrinspot, vonza, twoza, zig-zag-zav. Popti, vinaga, tin-li-tav. Harem, scarem, merchan tarem. Tier, tore . . .*

CHICOLINI is counted out. PINKY grins and points at him.

CHICOLINI : *I did it wrong. Wait, wait!* He points at BOB. *I start here. Rrrrrrinspot, vonza, twoza, zig-zag-zav. Popti, vinaga, tin-li-tav. Harem, scarem, merchan tarem. Tier, tore. . . .*

He counts himself out again. PINKY grins and points at him.

CHICOLINI : *'At'sa no good, too. Oh, I got it! I got it! Rrrrrrinspot, buck!*

He counts out PINKY, who looks bewildered as everyone shakes him vigorously by the hand.

FIREFLY : *You're a brave man. Go and break through the lines . . .* He lays a hand on his shoulder *. . . and remember, while you're out there risking life and limb, through shot and shell, we'll be in here thinking what a sucker you are!*

Cut to a medium shot.

FIREFLY : *Goodbye, Mont Blanc, goodbye.*

He makes the motion of kissing PINKY on both cheeks, while CHICHOLINI opens the door behind him. FIRELY turns to BOB, and PINKY snips off his raccoon tail with his scissors.

CHICOLINI saluting : *For Freedonia!*

BOB saluting : *For Freedonia!*

FIREFLY saluting : *For Freedonia!*

PINKY flourishes the scissors and falls backwards through the door . . .

And finds himself in the ammunition store. A shell whines over and explodes off-screen.

Out in the kitchen, the explosion brings a cartwheel chandelier

178

crashing down on Mrs Teasdale. Firefly runs up as she sinks to the ground.

Firefly : *Gloria! Gloria!*

She moans, and we cut in on the two of them as Firefly kneels beside her.

Firefly : *Where did they get you?*

She groans; we hear shots off-screen, while Firefly takes a jug of water from the table.

Bob and Chicolini are firing out of the window.

Chicolini : *Hey, careful with the water. It's the only water we got.*

Resume on Firefly and Mrs Teasdale. She groans.

Firefly : *Well, it's the only woman we got.* He splashes water on her face.

In the ammunition store, Pinky has been having a quiet smoke. He tosses his cigarette end away . . .

And it lands on some kegs of gunpowder. They explode.

Resume on Pinky, who struggles wildly, trying to open the door, as the ammunition starts exploding like fireworks all around him.

Long shot of the kitchen. Bob and Chicolini are at the window in the background. Firefly gets up from beside Mrs Teasdale and Chicolini follows him across to the door through which Pinky went out. We hear the ammunition exploding off-screen.

Firefly : *We're surrounded! They're attacking from the rear.*

Chicolini : *They're comin' this way.*

Firefly : *We'll barricade the door.*

Chicolini : *Come on, let's go.*

They start to barricade the door with a large cupboard.

Inside, Pinky is pounding at the door with the ammunition exploding all around him.

The pounding continues as we resume on the outside, where Firefly and Chicolini are piling things on top of the cupboard. A chair falls on Firefly's head from the top of the barricade.

Inside, Pinky struggles wildly amid more and more explosions. More pounding and explosions, heard from outside as Chicolini replaces the chair, while Firefly runs across to the wireless.

Shot of FIREFLY at the wireless.

FIREFLY : *This is Firefly talking. Send help at once.*

A voice answers from the wireless.

VOICE : *Help is on the way!*

Resume on CHICOLINI, holding up the barricade, as FIREFLY shouts, waving his arms.

FIREFLY : *Carry on, men, help is on the way!*

We see two fire engines driving out of a fire station with their sirens going, in a speeded up shot.

Then a troop of motorcycle police speeding along a road, also in fast motion. The engines roar; camera tracks ahead of them.

Marathon runners come towards us along a road, flanked by cheering spectators.

More cheering as camera pans with rowing eights on a river.

A line of swimmers leap into the water. More cheering.

Shot of some monkeys crossing a rope bridge over a jungle stream, howling.

A mother elephant and her baby thunder towards camera, seen in fast motion . . .

Then a whole herd of elephants, also speeded up, trumpeting as they go.

Resume on the howling monkeys . . .

The trumpeting elephants . . .

Then we see a whole school of porpoises leaping through the water in fast motion.

We see the Sylvanian soldiers again, firing from behind the row of sandbags.

Seen through a gap in the farmhouse wall, FIREFLY rises into view behind a palisade and looks to and fro. He has a large white bandage tied round his head with the ends sticking up like rabbit's ears.

Shot of the scene inside the house. CHICOLINI, FIREFLY and BOB are firing through part of the ruined wall, while MRS TEASDALE loads a gun in the foreground. A soldier rises from behind a palisade in the background and shoots FIREFLY in the backside. Then he ducks down again.

FIREFLY clutching his backside : *They got me! They got me! Water!*

We return to PINKY inside the ammunition store. As he tries

to break down the door, there is a loud explosion . . .

And PINKY is blown out into the room.

Resume on the others. FIREFLY is leaning back against the palisade while CHICOLINI pours water down his throat from the jug.

FIREFLY faintly : *Water!*

Outside the house, a Sylvanian soldier is seen from below as he climbs over the palisade.

We see him again from the inside — he has put his foot on the jug, which is now stuck over FIREFLY's head. BOB watches while CHICOLINI hits the soldier over the head with a brick and he falls back out of sight. FIREFLY gets up and calls in a muffled voice :

FIREFLY : *Get me out of this! Get me out of this!*

Resume on the Sylvanian soldiers behind the sandbags. They fire a volley.

While inside the house, FIREFLY and PINKY try to remove the jug from FIREFLY's head.

FIREFLY in a muffled voice : *The last time this happened to me, I was crawling under a bed.*

Shot of BOB and MRS TEASDALE aiming their guns over the palisade.

MRS TEASDALE : *Oh, if help would only come!*

Resume on FIREFLY and PINKY — who has painted a picture of FIREFLY's face on the jug. He lays down the barrel lid he has been using as a palette and admires his handiwork as BOB comes up and salutes.

BOB : *Your Excellency!*

Outside the house, the Sylvanian soldiers start jumping over the sandbag barricade.

Shot of FIREFLY, CHICOLINI and PINKY. PINKY strikes a match.

We see PINKY's hands lighting a firecracker.

PINKY puts the lighted firecracker inside the jug on FIREFLY's head. He and CHICOLINI take cover.

Cut to a closer shot; there is a loud explosion. The smoke clears away to reveal FIREFLY with the remains of the jug hanging round his neck.

FIREFLY : *Any mail for me while I was gone?*

Outside the house, the Sylvanian soldiers are now pounding on the door with a battering ram . . .

While inside CHICOLINI, BOB and MRS TEASDALE push furniture up against the door. PINKY pushes at MRS TEASDALE's backside.

MRS TEASDALE indignantly : *Get away! Get away from me!*

Resume on the soldiers pounding on the door.

Inside everyone stands back as the barricade falls down. MRS TEASDALE screams.

The soldiers start going in through the hole in the door.

On the other side, CHICOLINI, PINKY and BOB are waiting to receive them. CHICOLINI and BOB stand on either side of the door and CHICOLINI lifts the first soldier's tin helmet while PINKY hits him on the head with a brick. He staggers out of shot.

On the other side of the room, FIREFLY starts counting the heads — moving curtain rings along a pole slung from the ceiling with the bayonet on his rifle.

CHICOLINI and PINKY deal with the next soldier in the same way. He staggers off . . .

And FIREFLY moves another ring along the pole.

Resume on the scene at the door. CHICOLINI lifts the helmet of the next soldier and shouts :

CHICOLINI : *Hey! Trentino!*

They grab him, and we cut back to FIREFLY.

FIREFLY : *Trentino, eh? That's game.*

He shoves all the rings along the pole.

At the door, CHICOLINI and PINKY wedge TRENTINO's head in the broken door and exit.

Seen in a medium shot, FIREFLY, CHICOLINI, PINKY and BOB run up to the table. MRS TEASDALE is in the background.

CHICOLINI : *Trentino!*

FIREFLY : *Trentino, eh?*

They start throwing fruit.

FIREFLY : *Ahh! Call me an upstart, eh?*

We see TRENTINO as the fruit hits him with a thud, then cut to a closer shot as the bombardment continues.

TRENTINO shouting : *I surrender! I surrender!*

Back to FIREFLY and the others.

FIREFLY : *I'm sorry, you'll have to wait till the fruit runs out.*

They carry on throwing.

In the corner, MRS TEASDALE shouts joyfully :

MRS TEASDALE : *Victory is ours!*

We see the others again as MRS TEASDALE, in the background, breaks into triumphant song.

MRS TEASDALE piercingly, with arms upraised :

> *Hail, hail Freedonia,*
> *Land of the brave ...*

They all turn and start throwing fruit at her. Then the orchestra takes up the tune as the picture fades, and the words THE END appear.